THIS BOOK BELONGS TO

- -

Start Planning Your Trip To West Virginia

With so many wonderful things to do in West Virginia, the task of narrowing down a travel itinerary may seem daunting.

However, no matter which of the 50 attractions listed herein you choose to visit, there are no wrong choices.

To begin with, West Virginia is rich in history, culture, and loads of recreation.

Whether you prefer a camping trip with family or a girls'/guys' weekend with your friends, there is something to do for everyone.

From scenic nature trails to astounding caverns and art museums to dinner theatres, West Virginia is fraught with vacation destinations.

If you find yourself asking the question of what to do in West Virginia, you've come to the right place.

Below, you'll find a comprehensive list of scenic places, famous places, points of interest, and things to see all within the confines of the 35th state.

If you've never had the pleasure of traveling to West Virginia, strap in and get ready for an exciting ride.

Happy Adventure

Your feedback means a lot for us!

Please, Consider leaving us "5 stars" on your Amazon review.

Thank You!

L.P	PLACES TO GO	LOCATION	EST.	VISITED
1	NEW RIVER GORGE NATIONAL PARK	GLEN JEAN	1978	
2	BECKLEY EXHIBITION COAL MINE & YOUTH MUSEUM	BECKLEY	....	
3	APPALACHIAN GLASS	WESTON	....	
4	SNOWSHOE MOUNTAIN	SNOWSHOE	1974	
5	CRANBERRY MOUNTAIN NATURE CENTER	HILLSBORO	....	
6	GOVERNOR'S MANSION	CHARLESTON	1925	
7	WEST VIRGINIA MINE WARS MUSEUM	MATEWAN	2015	
8	THE MUSEUM OF AMERICAN GLASS	WESTON	1993	
9	MOTHMAN MUSEUM	POINT PLEASANT	....	
10	CHARLESTON CAPITOL MARKET	CHARLESTON	....	
11	MOUNTAIN RAIL ADVENTURES	ELKINS	....	
12	WEST VIRGINIA STATE MUSEUM	CHARLESTON	1894	
13	GRANDVIEW STATE PARK	BEAVER	1939	
14	GREEN BANK OBSERVATORY	GREEN BANK	1957	
15	LOST WORLD CAVERNS	LEWISBURG	1942	
16	WEST VIRGINIA BOTANIC GARDEN	MORGANTOWN	2000	
17	THE GREENBRIER	WHITE SULPHUR SPRINGS	1913	
18	HERITAGE FARM MUSEUM AND VILLAGE	HUNTINGTON	1996	
19	HARPERS FERRY	WV(U.S)	1732	
20	BLACKWATER FALLS STATE PARK	DAVIS	1937	
21	WEST VIRGINIA PENITENTIARY	MOUNDSVILLE	1876	
22	GREENBRIER STATE FOREST	CALDWELL	1938	
23	ACE ADVENTURE RESORT	OAK HILL	....	
24	SENECA ROCKS	WV(U.S)	1965	
25	SENECA CAVERNS	RIVERTON	1928	
26	LAKE SHAWNEE AMUSEMENT PARK	ROCK	1926	
27	KRUGER STREET TOY AND TRAIN MUSEUM	WHEELING	....	
28	DOLLY SODS WILDERNESS AREA	WV(U.S)	1975	
29	COOPERS ROCK STATE FOREST	BRUCETON MILLS	1936	
30	APPALACHIAN NATIONAL SCENIC TRAIL	HARPERS FERRY	1968	
31	ARTHURDALE HISTORIC DISTRICT	REEDSVILLE	1933	
32	MOUNTWOOD PARK	WAVERLY	1980	
33	TYGART LAKE STATE PARK	GRAFTON	1938	
34	TRANS-ALLEGHENY LUNATIC ASYLUM	WESTON	1858	
35	OGLEBAY RESORT	WHEELING	1928	
36	MOUNTAINEER FIELD	MORGANTOWN	1980	
37	CLAY CENTER FOR THE ARTS AND SCIENCES	CHARLESTON	2003	
38	GRAND VUE PARK	MOUNDSVILLE	....	
39	AUDRA STATE PARK	BUCKHANNON	1950	
40	BABCOCK STATE PARK	CLIFFTOP	1934	
41	BEARTOWN STATE PARK	RENICK	1970	
42	BERKELEY SPRINGS STATE PARK	BERKELEY SPRINGS	1970	
43	BLUESTONE STATE PARK	HINTON	1950	
44	CACAPON RESORT STATE PARK	BERKELEY SPRINGS	....	
45	CASS SCENIC RAILROAD STATE PARK	CASS	1961	
46	CEDAR CREEK STATE PARK	GLENVILLE	1955	
47	CHESAPEAKE & OHIO CANAL	WILLIAMSPORT	1828	
48	CHIEF LOGAN STATE PARK	LOGAN	1969	
49	HARPERS FERRY	WV(U.S)	1732	
50	GAULEY RIVER	GLEN JEAN	....	

Inventory

- [ ] Binoculars
- [ ] Bear Spray
- [ ] Cell Phone + Charger
- [ ] Camera + Accessories
- [ ] First aid kit
- [ ] Flashlight / Headlamp
- [ ] Fleece / Waterproof Jacket
- [ ] Guide Book
- [ ] Hand Lotion
- [ ] Hiking Shoes
- [ ] Hand Sanitizer
- [ ] Insect Repellent
- [ ] Lip Balm
- [ ] Medications & Painkillers
- [ ] Maps
- [ ] Ticket / Pass
- [ ] Snacks
- [ ] Sunglasses
- [ ] Spare Socks
- [ ] Sunscreen
- [ ] Sun Hat
- [ ] Trash Bags
- [ ] Toilet Paper
- [ ] Walking Stick
- [ ] Water

- [ ] Sport Shoes
- [ ] Swim Wear
- [ ] Towel
- [ ] Rainproof Backpack Cover
- [ ] Pendrive
- [ ] Powerbank
- [ ] Laptop
- [ ] Small Tripod
- [ ] Phone Holder
- [ ] Extender Cable
- [ ] Bulbs / Fuses
- [ ] Scissors
- [ ] Tent
- [ ] Trash Bags
- [ ] Umbrella
- [ ] National Park Maps
- [ ] National Park Maps
- [ ] Cosmetics
- [ ] Passport / Photocopy
- [ ] Id Card
- [ ] Driver's License
- [ ] ATM Cards
- [ ] Cash
- [ ] Green Card
- [ ] Tool Box

New River Gorge National Park

VISTED DATE :   SPRING ◯ SUMMER ◯ FALL ◯ WINTER ◯

WEATHER :   ☀◯ ⛅◯ 🌧◯ 🌨◯ ⛈◯ 🌬◯   🌡 TEMP :

FEE(S) :   RATING : ☆ ☆ ☆ ☆ ☆   WILL I RETURN?   YES / NO

LODGING :   WHO I WENT WITH :

DESCRIPTION / THINGS TO DO :

IF YOU'RE UNSURE OF WHAT TO DO IN WV, NEW RIVER GORGE NATIONAL PARK IS A WONDERFUL OPTION WITH LOADS OF OUTDOOR POSSIBILITIES.

NOTABLY, NEW RIVER IS ONE OF THE CONTINENT'S OLDEST RIVERS AND IT'S SURROUNDED BY MORE THAN 70,000 ACRES OF FORESTRY AND PARK.

THE CRAGGY, WHITEWATER RIVER FLOWS THROUGH PITTED CANYONS AND IS THE SCENE OF PLENTY OF SEASONAL FUN.

LIKE NEW RIVER, THE PARK ITSELF PROVIDES LIMITLESS OPPORTUNITIES FOR SCENIC ADVENTURES.

IF YOU'RE INTERESTED IN A MORE LEISURELY EXPERIENCE, YOU MIGHT CONSIDER CAMPING, A SCENIC DRIVE, FISHING, OR BICYCLING. IF YOU'RE LOOKING FOR MORE ACTION-PACKED EXCITEMENT, VISITORS ARE WELCOME TO CLIMB, HIKE, HUNT, AND EVEN WHITEWATER RAFT.

BUT NO MATTER HOW YOU PLAN TO SPEND YOUR TIME HERE, THE FOCAL POINT FOR ALL VISITORS IS ALWAYS THE NEW RIVER GORGE BRIDGE, A STRUCTURAL MASTERPIECE THAT IS THE MOST PHOTOGRAPHED SITE IN ALL OF WEST VIRGINIA.

SO, IF YOU'RE WONDERING WHAT TO DO IN WV, WONDER NO MORE; PLAN TO SPEND SOME TIME IN THIS MAGNIFICENT PARK.

ADDRESS: GLEN JEAN, WV 25846, UNITED STATES

PASSPORT STAMPS:

NOTES :

Beckley Exhibition Coal Mine and Youth Museum

VISTED DATE : SPRING ◯ SUMMER ◯ FALL ◯ WINTER ◯

WEATHER : ☀ ◯ ⛅ ◯ 🌧 ◯ 🌨 ◯ ⛈ ◯ 💨 ◯ 🌡 TEMP :

FEE(S) : RATING : ☆ ☆ ☆ ☆ ☆ WILL I RETURN? YES / NO

LODGING : WHO I WENT WITH :

DESCRIPTION / THINGS TO DO :

ONE OF MANY UNIQUE THINGS TO DO IN WV IS THE BECKLEY EXHIBITION COAL MINE AND YOUTH MUSEUM. DURING YOUR COAL MINE TOUR, YOU WILL SEE THE UNDERGROUND MINE AND VISIT AN OLD COAL CAMP.

THIS INTERACTIVE AND HISTORICAL TOUR WILL GIVE YOU A FEEL FOR LIFE AS A COAL MINER. RIDING THE DARK PASSAGEWAYS OF THE OLD COAL MINE IS A ONCE-IN-A-LIFETIME EXPERIENCE.

NOTABLY, THE TOURS ARE GUIDED BY VETERAN COAL MINERS WHO SHARE FIRSTHAND STORIES OF THEIR EXPERIENCES AND RESPONSIBILITIES AS MINERS. AFTER YOUR MINE TOUR, YOU'LL ALSO ENJOY VISITING - THE YOUTH MUSEUM, WHICH FEATURES INTERACTIVE EXHIBITS FOR CHILDREN.

WITH EXHIBITS ON THE SOLAR SYSTEM, THE APPALACHIAN FRONTIER, AND RECONSTRUCTED HISTORICAL BUILDINGS, YOUR LITTLE ONE WILL LOVE LEARNING ALL ABOUT WEST VIRGINIA HISTORY.

KNOWLEDGEABLE TOUR GUIDES EXCITEDLY SHARE THE SIGNIFICANCE OF EACH BUILDING IN AN ENGAGING AND INFORMATIVE WAY.

WHAT'S MORE, THE PROPERTY IS SITUATED UPON A METICULOUSLY KEPT LANDSCAPE; VERDANT LAWNS, COLORFUL FLOWERS, AND PICNIC AREAS ARE THE BACKDROP TO YOUR TOUR OF THE PROPERTY. FINALLY, THERE IS ALSO A WONDERFUL GIFT SHOP ON PREMISES THAT SELLS SOUVENIRS, WEST VIRGINIA NOVEL-TIES, AND HOMEMADE FUDGE. BE SURE TO CHECK OUT THIS TOP SIGHTSEEING ATTRACTION IN WV.

ADDRESS: 513 EWART AVE, BECKLEY, WV 25801, UNITED STATES

PASSPORT STAMPS:

NOTES :

Appalachian Glass

VISTED DATE :   SPRING ◯   SUMMER ◯   FALL ◯   WINTER ◯

WEATHER :   ☀ ◯   ⛅ ◯   🌧 ◯   🌨 ◯   ⛈ ◯   🌬 ◯   🌡 TEMP :

FEE(S) :   RATING : ☆ ☆ ☆ ☆ ☆   WILL I RETURN?   YES / NO

LODGING :   WHO I WENT WITH :

DESCRIPTION / THINGS TO DO :

HOME TO THREE GENERATIONS OF TALENTED GLASSMAKERS, APPALACHIAN GLASS IS A FUN PLACE TO VISIT IN WEST VIRGINIA.

MATT, CHIP, AND TODD TURNER ARE THE ARTISTS BEHIND THE BEAUTIFUL GLASS PIECES YOU'LL ENCOUNTER DURING YOUR VISIT.

THIS FAMILY OF GLASSBLOWERS HAS WORKED TOGETHER, OFTENTIMES LEARNING FROM EACH OTHER, TO CRAFT BOTH BEAUTIFUL AND FUNCTIONAL GLASS WITH MORE THAN 75 YEARS OF COMBINED INDUSTRY EXPERIENCE.

BECAUSE WEST VIRGINIA IS RICH IN THE NATURAL RESOURCES NECESSARY TO MAKE GLASS, THESE FELLOWS WERE LUCKY TO FIND THEIR CALLING WHERE THEY DID. OF NOTE, APPALACHIAN GLASS PROVIDES DAILY GLASS BLOWING DEMONSTRATIONS; IF YOU'VE NEVER SEEN THIS DONE IN PERSON, IT'S A SIGHT TO BEHOLD!

THE PROCESS ROUGHLY INCLUDES BLOWING AIR INTO A GLOB OF MOLTEN GLASS WHILE ROLLING IT TO THE DESIRED SHAPE; THIS PROCESS IS REPEATED UNTIL THE FINAL PRODUCT IS ACHIEVED AND THEN IT'S PLACED IN A KILN FOR IT TO SET.

THE PROCESS IS INTRICATE, DELICATE, AND REQUIRES THE TYPE OF FINESSE THAT ONLY MANY YEARS OF EXPERIENCE PRODUCES. THIS WEST VIRGINIA HOT SPOT (PUN INTENDED) IS A MUST SEE; YOU WON'T BE DISAPPOINTED.

ADDRESS: 499 US-33, WESTON, WV 26452, UNITED STATES

PASSPORT STAMPS:

NOTES :

Snowshoe Mountain

VISTED DATE :   SPRING ◯ SUMMER ◯ FALL ◯ WINTER ◯

WEATHER :   ☀ ◯ ⛅ ◯ 🌧 ◯ 🌨 ◯ ⛈ ◯ 🌬 ◯   🌡 TEMP :

FEE(S) :   RATING : ☆ ☆ ☆ ☆ ☆   WILL I RETURN?   YES / NO

LODGING :   WHO I WENT WITH :

DESCRIPTION / THINGS TO DO :

WHETHER YOU'RE LOOKING FOR PLACES TO GO WHEN VISITING WEST VIRGINIA IN THE WINTER OR SUMMER MONTHS, BE SURE TO VISIT SNOWSHOE MOUNTAIN.

THIS MOUNTAIN RESORT COUPLES ACTION-PACKED SNOW ADVENTURES WITH POSH COMFORT AND LUXURY. AT SNOWSHOE MOUNTAIN VISITORS CAN SKI, SNOWBOARD, SNOWMOBILE, AND/OR LEARN IT ALL AT SKI SCHOOL.

WHEN THE WEATHER WARMS UP, SNOWSHOE SWITCHES GEARS TO ALL-TERRAIN MOUNTAIN ADVENTURES. VISITORS CAN MOUNTAIN BIKE, HIKE, CANOE/KAYAK ON THE LAKE, STAND-UP PADDLEBOARD, DO SEGWAY TOURS, GOLF, AND MORE.

THANKFULLY, NO MATTER THE TIME OF YEAR, SNOWSHOE MOUNTAIN IS READY TO DELIVER BIG THRILLS. FURTHERMORE, WHEN YOU'RE READY TO WIND DOWN FOR THE DAY OR NIGHT, THE RESORT IS READY FOR YOU.

WITH WORLD-CLASS DINING OPTIONS LIKE A MOUNTAIN-TOP RESTAURANT, YOU'LL BE SATISFIED AFTER EVERY MEAL. MOREOVER, SNOWSHOE'S NEARBY VILLAGE IS HOME TO SOME OF THE MOST POPULAR RE-STAURANTS AND SHOPPING YOU CAN IMAGINE.

THIS TOP VACATION SPOT, NO MATTER THE SEASON, IS ONE OF THE TOP 10 THINGS TO DO IN WEST VIRGINIA, SO BE SURE TO BOOK YOUR RESERVATIONS NOW.

ADDRESS: 10 SNOWSHOE DR, SNOWSHOE, WV 26209, UNITED STATES

PASSPORT STAMPS:

NOTES :

Cranberry Mountain Nature Center

VISTED DATE :   SPRING ◯   SUMMER ◯   FALL ◯   WINTER ◯

WEATHER :   ☀️◯   ⛅◯   🌧️◯   🌨️◯   ⛈️◯   🌬️◯   🌡️TEMP :

FEE(S) :   RATING : ☆ ☆ ☆ ☆ ☆   WILL I RETURN?   YES / NO

LODGING :   WHO I WENT WITH :

DESCRIPTION / THINGS TO DO :

THIS DESTINATION IS PART OF THE MONONGAHELA NATIONAL FOREST IN WEST VIRGINIA AND IS ONE OF THE STATE'S TOP VACATION SPOTS. THE CRANBERRY MOUNTAIN NATURE CENTER IS HOME TO AN EXHIBIT HALL THAT FEATURES MANY HANDS-ON DISPLAYS.

APPEALING TO CHILDREN AND ADULTS ALIKE, THE EXHIBITS ARE FUN, ENTERTAINING, AND BEST OF ALL EDUCATIONAL. THE CENTER'S AUDITORIUM SHOWS ENGAGING FILMS ON TOPICS LIKE SMOKEY THE BEAR, WILDFLOWERS, AND MORE.

THE CENTER ALSO HOSTS MANY-FACETED EVENTS THROUGHOUT THE YEAR LIKE KIDS' NIGHTS, LIVE SNAKE SHOWS, WILDLIFE DEMONSTRATIONS, AND BEYOND.

WHAT'S MORE, CRANBERRY MOUNTAIN NATURE CENTER ALSO DELIVERS PROGRAMS ON TOPICS IMPORTANT TO THE STATE LIKE THE DIFFERENCES BETWEEN POISONOUS AND NONPOISONOUS - SNAKES AND TOURS OF THE CRANBERRY GLADES.

FINALLY, ANOTHER OF THE CENTER'S FAVORED ATTRACTIONS IS THE NATURE STORE WHERE VISITORS CAN PURCHASE NATURE GUIDES, FOLKLORE BOOKS, COOKBOOKS, CLOTHING, POSTCARDS, AND MORE.

WEST VIRGINIA, NOT SHORT ON PLACES TO SEE, IS HOME TO THIS MUST SEE NATURE CENTER.

ADDRESS: INTERSECTION OF RT 39/55 AND, WV-150, HILLSBORO, WV 24946, UNITED STATES

PASSPORT STAMPS:

NOTES :

Governor's Mansion

VISTED DATE :		SPRING ◯ SUMMER ◯ FALL ◯ WINTER ◯

WEATHER : ☀◯ ⛅◯ 🌧◯ 🌨◯ ⛈◯ 🌬◯   🌡 TEMP :

FEE(S) :	RATING : ☆ ☆ ☆ ☆ ☆	WILL I RETURN? YES / NO

LODGING :	WHO I WENT WITH :

DESCRIPTION / THINGS TO DO :

ONE OF THE MOST BEAUTIFUL PLACES IN THE USA, THE WEST VIRGINIA GOVERNOR'S MANSION IS A WONDERFUL SIGHTSEEING DESTINATION. THIS LANDMARK IS SITUATED IN THE STATE'S CAPITOL AND HAS BEEN HOME TO WEST VIRGINIA GOVERNORS SINCE 1925.

BEYOND HOUSING THE STATE'S MOST ESTEEMED OFFICIAL, THE MANSION HAS ALSO WELCOMED FOREIGN AND DOMESTIC DIGNITARIES ALIKE.

BUT BEYOND THE HIGH-PROFILE MANSION RESIDENTS AND GUESTS IS THE ARCHITECTURE, DECOR, AND LANDSCAPE OF THE MANSION; THESE ARE THE REAL DRAWS FOR VISITORS.

SOME NOTABLE DESIGN FEATURES INCLUDE A MARBLE CHECKERBOARD FOYER FLOOR, DRAWING-ROOM WALLS PAINTED IN A UNIQUE OPTICAL ILLUSION, AND INCREDIBLE LANDSCAPING.

TOURING THE WEST VIRGINIA GOVERNOR'S MANSION IS AN EXCELLENT ATTRACTION FOR BOTH HISTORY AND ARCHITECTURE ENTHUSIASTS.

THE WELL-CARED-FOR PROPERTY AND HISTORY-RICH DESIGN FEATURES MAKE THE MANSION ONE OF THE COOLEST PLACES TO SEE IN THE STATE.

ALTHOUGH TOURS ARE FREE, THEY DO REQUIRE A RESERVATION AS TOURS ARE ONLY GIVEN ON THURSDAYS AND FRIDAYS.

ADDRESS: 1716 KANAWHA BLVD E, CHARLESTON, WV 25305, UNITED STATES

PASSPORT STAMPS:

NOTES :

West Virginia Mine Wars Museum

VISTED DATE :   SPRING ○ SUMMER ○ FALL ○ WINTER ○

WEATHER : ☀ ○ ⛅ ○ 🌧 ○ 🌨 ○ ⛈ ○ 🌬 ○   🌡 TEMP :

FEE(S) :   RATING : ☆ ☆ ☆ ☆ ☆   WILL I RETURN? YES / NO

LODGING :   WHO I WENT WITH :

DESCRIPTION / THINGS TO DO :

HOME TO A SLICE OF UNSETTLING AMERICAN HISTORY, THE WEST VIRGINIA MINE WARS MUSEUM PRESERVES ARTIFACTS SURROUNDING ONE OF THE LARGEST CIVIL UPRISINGS SINCE THE CIVIL WAR, THE MINE WARS.

ESSENTIALLY, THE MINE WARS WERE TURF WARS BETWEEN UNIONIZED MINERS AND COAL MINES.

THE PURPOSE OF THE MUSEUM IS TO UPHOLD THE VOICES OF THOSE INVOLVED, THOSE WHO MADE THE ULTIMATE SACRIFICE, AND THE TRIUMPHANT. INSIDE THE MUSEUM IS THE COUNTRY'S LARGEST COLLECTION OF MINE WARS MEMORABILIA.

VISITORS ARE GIVEN GUIDED TOURS OF THINGS LIKE LIFE IN COAL CAMPS, LOCAL COAL STRIKES, AND COAL MINERS' TOOLS AND LIFESTYLES.

NOTABLY, THROUGH THESE ARTIFACTS, THE WEST VIRGINIA MINE WARS MUSEUM CELEBRATES A FRIGHTENING YET TRIUMPHANT TIME IN AMERICAN HISTORY.

ONCE YOU'VE COMPLETED THIS INTERESTING TOUR, BE SURE TO CHECK OUT THE MUSEUM'S GIFT SHOP WHICH SELLS APPAREL AND NIFTY SOUVENIRS.

FINALLY, IF YOU'RE TRAVELING WITH HISTORY BUFFS, THEY'LL CERTAINLY ENJOY THIS INTERESTING WEST VIRGINIA ATTRACTION.

ADDRESS: 401 MATE ST, MATEWAN, WV 25678, UNITED STATES

PASSPORT STAMPS:

NOTES :

The Museum of American Glass

VISTED DATE :   SPRING ○   SUMMER ○   FALL ○   WINTER ○

WEATHER :   ☀ ○   ⛅ ○   🌧 ○   🌨 ○   ⛈ ○   🌬 ○   🌡 TEMP :

FEE(S) :   RATING : ☆ ☆ ☆ ☆ ☆   WILL I RETURN?   YES / NO

LODGING :   WHO I WENT WITH :

DESCRIPTION / THINGS TO DO :

AS NOTED EARLIER, GLASS IS ONE OF WEST VIRGINIA'S RICHEST RESOURCES.

AS SUCH, THE MUSEUM OF AMERICAN GLASS CELEBRATES THE REGION'S RICH GLASS HERITAGE.

ESTABLISHED IN 1933, THE MUSEUM AIMS TO SHARE GLASS PIECES AND ARTIST STORIES SPECIFIC TO WEST VIRGINIA.

IN ADDITION TO SEEING AN ASSORTMENT OF UNIQUE EARLY PERIOD PIECES, KITCHEN GLASS, LAMPS, NOVELTIES, AND HUNDREDS MORE, THE VAST MUSEUM COLLECTIONS ARE ASTOUNDING. THE MUSEUM ALSO HOSTS EVER-CHANGING TRAVELING EXHIBITS THAT ARE SURE TO WOW YOU.

FURTHERMORE, THE MUSEUM FREQUENTLY HOSTS SPECIAL PROGRAMMING LIKE GLASS COLLECTING CLUBS AND SPECIALTY GLASS SHOWS. BE SURE TO CHECK OUT THE MUSEUM'S CALENDAR OF EVENTS TO SEE IF ANYTHING SPECIAL IS HAPPENING DURING YOUR VISIT.

FOLLOWING YOUR TOUR OF THIS COMPREHENSIVE HOMAGE TO THE WEST VIRGINIA GLASS HERITAGE, THE MUSEUM GIFT SHOP WELCOMES YOU TO PERUSE MONOGRAPHS, CATALOGS, AND COLLECTIBLES.

IF YOU'RE LOOKING FOR UNIQUE PLACES TO GO IN WEST VIRGINIA THIS WEEKEND, BE SURE TO GIVE THE MUSEUM OF AMERICAN GLASS A GANDER.

ADDRESS: 230 MAIN AVE, WESTON, WV 26452, UNITED STATES

PASSPORT STAMPS:

NOTES :

Mothman Museum

VISTED DATE :   SPRING ○ SUMMER ○ FALL ○ WINTER ○

WEATHER : ☀ ○ ⛅ ○ 🌧 ○ 🌨 ○ ⛈ ○ 🌬 ○   🌡 TEMP :

FEE(S) :   RATING : ☆ ☆ ☆ ☆ ☆   WILL I RETURN? YES / NO

LODGING :   WHO I WENT WITH :

DESCRIPTION / THINGS TO DO :

PROBABLY ONE OF THE CREEPIEST THINGS TO DO IN WV, THE MOTHMAN MUSEUM PAYS TRIBUTE TO A SERIES OF STRANGE EVENTS THAT AFFLICTED THE SMALL TOWN OF POINT PLEASANT.

WITH THE COMMENCEMENT OF STRANGE SIGHTINGS LIKE DISTURBING LIGHTS IN THE SKY, PECULIAR "MEN IN BLACK," AND A RED-EYED LIFE FORM NOW KNOWN AS MOTHMAN, RESIDENTS OF THE SMALL TOWN WERE MYSTIFIED. THE MUSEUM PAYS HOMAGE TO THESE STRANGE OCCURRENCES.

NOTABLY, THE MUSEUM SHARES EXPERTLY DISPLAYED CASES OF NEWS ARTICLES, PHOTOGRAPHS, RECORDINGS, AND MORE SURROUNDING THE INCIDENTS.

ADDITIONALLY, THE MUSEUM HOUSES MOTHMAN ART, COMICS, COSTUMES, REPLICAS, AND A WIDE ARRAY OF ARTIFACTS.

WHETHER YOU'RE FAMILIAR WITH THE STRANGE STORY OF MOTHMAN OR YOU'RE JUST FASCINATED BY ODDITIES, YOU'RE SURE TO LOVE YOUR VISIT TO MOTHMAN MUSEUM.

BEST OF ALL, THE MUSEUM'S GIFT SHOP HAS THE WORLD'S LARGEST AND MOST ECLECTIC COLLECTION OF MOTHMAN SOUVENIRS AND MEMORABILIA.

LASTLY, THERE ARE STILL SO MANY QUESTIONS SURROUNDING WHO OR WHAT MOTHMAN IS/WAS, BUT THERE'S NO QUESTION THAT YOU'LL LOVE VISITING THIS STRANGE WEST VIRGINIA ATTRACTION.

ADDRESS: 400 MAIN ST, POINT PLEASANT, WV 25550, UNITED STATES

PASSPORT STAMPS:

NOTES :

Charleston Capitol Market

VISTED DATE :   SPRING ◯   SUMMER ◯   FALL ◯   WINTER ◯

WEATHER :   ☀️◯   ⛅◯   🌧️◯   🌨️◯   ⛈️◯   🌬️◯   🌡️ TEMP :

FEE(S) :   RATING : ☆ ☆ ☆ ☆ ☆   WILL I RETURN?   YES / NO

LODGING :   WHO I WENT WITH :

DESCRIPTION / THINGS TO DO :

ESTABLISHED MORE THAN 20 YEARS AGO, CHARLESTON CAPITOL MARKET IS A WEST VIRGINIA INSTITUTION.

A ONCE MODEST FARMER'S MARKET, TODAY THE MARKET IS AN INDOOR AND OUTDOOR SHOPPING AND SOCIAL SCENE.

NOW ONE OF MANY PREMIER TOURIST ATTRACTIONS, CHARLESTON CAPITOL MARKET IS HOME TO INDOOR MERCHANTS SPECIALIZING IN SUCH THINGS AS CHEESE/WINE, FINE CHOCOLATES, SUSHI, ITALIAN DELECTABLES, COFFEE SPECIALTIES, AND SO MUCH MORE.

YOU'LL FIND PURVEYORS OF FARM GOODS, BOTANICALS, LANDSCAPING, AND PRODUCE GALORE IN THE OUTDOOR MARKET. BEYOND ALL OF THE WONDERFULLY DELIGHTFUL MERCHANTS AND GOODS YOU'LL ENCOUNTER, THE MARKET FREQUENTLY HOSTS SPECIAL EVENTS LIKE MARKET MIXERS, COOK-OFFS, AND MORE.

BEST OF ALL, THE MARKET IS OPEN YEAR-ROUND SELLING SEASONAL GOODS TO LOCALS AND VISITORS ALIKE. FINALLY, SEASONAL EVENTS LIKE CHRISTMAS TREE AND PUMPKIN PICKING, GARDEN PLANNING, AND PICNIC SHOPPING ARE OTHER LOVELY MARKET FEATURES.

IF YOU'RE LOOKING FOR AMUSING THINGS TO SEE IN WEST VIRGINIA, MAKE SURE TO STOP BY CHARLESTON CAPITOL MARKET.

ADDRESS: 800 SMITH ST, CHARLESTON, WV 25301, UNITED STATES

PASSPORT STAMPS:

NOTES :

Mountain Rail Adventures

VISTED DATE :   SPRING ◯   SUMMER ◯   FALL ◯   WINTER ◯

WEATHER :   ☀️◯   ⛅◯   🌧️◯   🌨️◯   ⛈️◯   🌬️◯   🌡️ TEMP :

FEE(S) :   RATING : ☆ ☆ ☆ ☆ ☆   WILL I RETURN?   YES / NO

LODGING :   WHO I WENT WITH :

DESCRIPTION / THINGS TO DO :

IF YOU'RE LOOKING TO ENJOY THE BEST OF SCENIC WEST VIRGINIA AND THE HISTORIC LORE AND CHARM OF CLASSIC TRAINS, THIS TOP ATTRACTION IS FOR YOU.

THINGS TO DO IN WEST VIRGINIA AREN'T HARD TO COME BY, BUT THIS TOP EXPERIENCE IS ONE OF THE BEST. UPON THE CASS SCENIC RAILROAD, VISITORS RIDE OLD-TIMEY STEAM LOCOMOTIVES.

DURING THEIR RIDE ON THE SHAY LOCOMOTIVE, PASSENGERS DELIGHT IN THE INCREASING SPEED OF THE ENGINES AGAINST THE BACKDROP OF SCENIC AND REMOTE EXPANSES OF WEST VIRGINIA.

NOTABLY, PASSENGERS WILL CHOOSE FROM ONE OF TWO AWESOME RAIL RIDES. DURING THE BALD KNOB TOUR, GUESTS WILL BASQUE IN THE 4-HOUR RIDE TO BALD KNOB, THE SECOND HIGHEST PEAK IN WV.

THE WHITTAKER STATION TOUR IS ONLY A 2-HOUR RIDE, THOUGH EQUALLY PICTURESQUE TO THE LATTER TOUR. NO MATTER THE TOUR YOU CHOOSE, BOTH ARE THRILLING AND UNFORGETTABLE.

ONE OF THE COOLEST WEST VIRGINIA ATTRACTIONS, A RIDE WITH MOUNTAIN RAIL ADVENTURES IS A TRULY MEMORABLE EXPERIENCE THAT YOU'LL NEVER FORGET.

ADDRESS: 315 RAILROAD AVE, ELKINS, WV 26241, UNITED STATES

PASSPORT STAMPS:

NOTES :

West Virginia State Museum

VISTED DATE : SPRING ◯ SUMMER ◯ FALL ◯ WINTER ◯

WEATHER : ☀ ◯ ⛅ ◯ 🌧 ◯ 🌨 ◯ ⛈ ◯ 🌬 ◯   🌡 TEMP :

FEE(S) :   RATING : ☆ ☆ ☆ ☆ ☆   WILL I RETURN? YES / NO

LODGING :   WHO I WENT WITH :

DESCRIPTION / THINGS TO DO :

LOCATED WITHIN THE WEST VIRGINIA CULTURAL CENTER, THE WEST VIRGINIA STATE MUSEUM RETRACES AND SHARES THE UNIQUE HISTORY OF THE STATE AS A WHOLE.

HOUSING SUCH ARTIFACTS AS ANTIQUE HATS TO A TELESCOPE USED BY AN AMERICAN PRESIDENT, THIS UNIQUE LOOK AT THE 35TH STATE IS ONE OF THE BEST PLACES TO VISIT IN WEST VIRGINIA.

OF NOTE, THE CHRONOLOGICAL LAYOUT OF THE MUSEUM'S EXHIBITS ALLOWS VISITORS TO CONCEPTUALIZE THE STATE'S EVOLUTION.

ESSENTIALLY, THE SPECIAL EXHIBITS RECREATE THE STATE'S HISTORY THROUGH NARRATION, SOUNDS, ILLUSTRATIONS, DESCRIPTIONS, AND MOST IMPORTANTLY SIGNIFICANT ARTIFACTS.

FURTHERMORE, THROUGH THE THOUGHT-PROVOKING DISPLAYS VISITORS WILL HAVE A BETTER UNDERSTANDING OF WEST VIRGINIA'S CULTURAL, INDUSTRIAL, AND NATURAL HISTORIES.

WEST VIRGINIA STATE MUSEUM IS A UNIQUE LENS THROUGH WHICH TO EXPERIENCE THE STATE.

BEST OF ALL, TOURS ARE FREE TO THE PUBLIC AND ONE OF MANY COOL PLACES TO VISIT WITH FRIENDS AND FAMILY.

ADDRESS: 1900 KANAWHA BLVD E #435, CHARLESTON, WV 25305, UNITED STATES

PASSPORT STAMPS:

NOTES :

Grandview State Park

VISTED DATE : SPRING ◯ SUMMER ◯ FALL ◯ WINTER ◯

WEATHER : ☀ ◯ ⛅ ◯ 🌧 ◯ 🌨 ◯ ⛈ ◯ 🌬 ◯ 🌡 TEMP :

FEE(S) : RATING : ☆ ☆ ☆ ☆ ☆ WILL I RETURN? YES / NO

LODGING : WHO I WENT WITH :

DESCRIPTION / THINGS TO DO :

IF YOU'RE UNSURE OF WHERE TO VISIT WHEN IN WEST VIRGINIA, BE SURE TO SPEND SOME TIME IN GRANDVIEW STATE PARK.

ONE OF THE MOST BEAUTIFUL PLACES TO VISIT IN THE STATE, THE PARK IS THE PERFECT SETTING FOR SIGHTSEEING, LEISURE, AND OUTDOOR ACTIVITIES.

ONE OF THE PARK'S MOST POPULAR PLACES OF INTEREST IS A SCENIC OVERLOOK THAT LOOKS UPON THE OUTSTANDING SIGHTS OF NEW RIVER, AN ACTIVE RAILWAY, AND THE VERDANT LANDSCAPE OF THE PARK.

TO REACH THE OVERLOOK, HIKERS WILL TRAVERSE THROUGH GORGEOUS RHODODENDRONS AND OTHER COLORFUL PLANT LIFE.

IN ADDITION TO THE BEAUTIFUL VIEWS AT GRANDVIEW STATE PARK, THERE ARE PLENTY OF OPPORTUNITIES FOR OUTDOOR FUN.

FOR INSTANCE, THE PARK HAS FIVE HIKING TRAILS WHICH MAY BE FOLLOWED ALONE OR WITH A RANGER-LED GUIDE. IN THE SUMMER, THE PARK HOSTS OUTDOOR THEATRE PRODUCTIONS.

FINALLY, ANY TIME OF YEAR IS A GOOD TIME TO PICNIC OR VISIT THE PARK'S PLAYGROUNDS. WITH SO MANY OUTDOOR ATTRACTIONS IN ONE PLACE, GRANDVIEW STATE PARK IS A GREAT PLACE TO VISIT DURING YOUR STAY IN WEST VIRGINIA.

ADDRESS: GRANDVIEW RD, BEAVER, WV 25813, UNITED STATES

PASSPORT STAMPS:

NOTES :

Green Bank Observatory

VISTED DATE : SPRING ◯ SUMMER ◯ FALL ◯ WINTER ◯

WEATHER : ☀ ◯ ⛅ ◯ ☁ ◯ 🌨 ◯ ⛈ ◯ 🌬 ◯   🌡 TEMP :

FEE(S) :   RATING : ☆ ☆ ☆ ☆ ☆   WILL I RETURN?   YES / NO

LODGING :   WHO I WENT WITH :

DESCRIPTION / THINGS TO DO :

LOCATED IN A NATIONAL QUIET ZONE, THE GREEN BANK OBSERVATORY PROVIDES ACCESS TO CUTTING-EDGE TELESCOPES AND FACILITIES FOR THE ASTRONOMICAL COMMUNITY. NOTABLY, THE OBSERVATORY IS AN INTERNATIONALLY RECOGNIZED LEADER IN RESEARCH AND EDUCATION.

WHEN ASTRONOMERS COME TO GREEN BANK OBSERVATORY, THEY LISTEN TO THE "REMOTE WHISPERS OF THE UNIVERSE." GREEN BANK OBSERVATORY PROVIDES THEM WITH THE FACILITY AND TECHNOLOGY TO SUCCESSFULLY DO SO.

THE OBSERVATORY IS OPEN TO THE PUBLIC FOR SPECIAL PRIVATE TOURS BUT RESERVATIONS AND SCREENINGS ARE REQUIRED. IF YOU SUCCESSFULLY PASS THE SITE'S SCREENING PROTOCOL, YOU WILL HAVE THE ONCE-IN-A-LIFETIME OPPORTUNITY TO TOUR THE FACILITY'S PRIVATE LABORATORIES, SEE THE MOST TECHNOLOGICALLY ADVANCED TELESCOPES, AND CHECK OUT FABRICATION SPACES.

THE OBSERVATORY ALSO HOSTS PUBLIC TOURS OF THE FACILITY WHEREIN YOU CAN CHECK OUT THE POPULAR CATCHING THE WAVE EXHIBIT HALL OR CATCH AN EDUCATIONAL FLICK IN THE AUDITORIUM.

FINISH YOUR DAY OFF WITH A BITE TO EAT IN THE STARLIGHT CAFE AND SOME LIGHT SHOPPING IN THE GIFT SHOP.

THIS MUST DO EXPERIENCE IS A FASCINATING WEST VIRGINIA ACTIVITY FOR THE WHOLE FAMILY.

ADDRESS: 155 OBSERVATORY RD, GREEN BANK, WV 24944, UNITED STATES

PASSPORT STAMPS:

NOTES :

Lost World Caverns

VISTED DATE :   SPRING ○   SUMMER ○   FALL ○   WINTER ○

WEATHER : ☀ ○   ⛅ ○   🌧 ○   🌨 ○   ⛈ ○   🌬 ○   🌡 TEMP :

FEE(S) :   RATING : ☆ ☆ ☆ ☆ ☆   WILL I RETURN?   YES / NO

LODGING :   WHO I WENT WITH :

DESCRIPTION / THINGS TO DO :

SITUATED 120-FEEL BENEATH THE EARTH'S SURFACE IS THE LOST WORLD CAVERNS IN WEST VIRGINIA.

PROBABLY ONE OF THE MOST MAGICAL PLACES TO VISIT IN WEST VIRGINIA, THE CAVERNS ARE HOME TO ASTOUNDING ROCK FORMATIONS. VISITORS ARE WELCOME TO EXPLORE THE FORMATIONS IN SELF-GUIDED TOURS THAT LEAD TOURISTS THROUGH A HALF-MILE CIRCLE.

THROUGHOUT THE TOUR, YOU'LL COME FACE TO FACE WITH SOME OF THE WORLD'S LARGEST AND MOST MAGNIFICENT STALACTITES AND OTHER CRYSTAL FORMATIONS.

ONE OF THIS ATTRACTION'S MOST POPULAR FEATURES IS THE "BRIDAL VEIL" WHICH IS A 28-FOOT STALAGMITE THAT YOU HAVE TO SEE IN PERSON TO BELIEVE. THANKFULLY, PHOTOGRAPHY IS PERMITTED IN THE CAVERNS BECAUSE THERE ARE MANY AMAZING PHOTO OPPORTUNITIES.

IN TOTAL, THE TOUR LASTS ABOUT 45 MINUTES, BUT THE MEMORIES WILL CERTAINLY LAST A LIFETIME. IN ADDITION TO THE CAVERN TOUR, YOU MAY ALSO PERUSE THE PROPERTY'S NATURAL HISTORY MUSEUM TO LEARN ABOUT INTERESTING PREHISTORIC CAVE-DWELLERS.

LOST WORLD CAVERNS ALSO HOSTS GEM MINING TOURS WHERE YOU'LL HAVE THE OPPORTUNITY TO FIND AND KEEP SEMI-PRECIOUS GEMSTONES, ARROWHEADS, ANCIENT FOSSILS, AND OTHER UNIQUE TREASURES. THE SIGHTS AT THIS WEST VIRGINIA ATTRACTION MAKE IT A PLACE YOU'VE GOT TO SEE DURING YOUR TRIP.

ADDRESS: 907 LOST WORLD RD, LEWISBURG, WV 24901, UNITED STATES

PASSPORT STAMPS:

NOTES :

West Virginia Botanic Garden

VISTED DATE :   SPRING ◯ SUMMER ◯ FALL ◯ WINTER ◯

WEATHER : ☀ ◯ 🌥 ◯ 🌧 ◯ 🌨 ◯ ⛈ ◯ 🌬 ◯   🌡 TEMP :

FEE(S) :   RATING : ☆ ☆ ☆ ☆ ☆   WILL I RETURN? YES / NO

LODGING :   WHO I WENT WITH :

DESCRIPTION / THINGS TO DO :

ONE OF MANY SCENIC THINGS TO DO IN WEST VIRGINIA, THIS GARDEN IS AN AMAZING SIGHT TO BEHOLD.

SITUATED ON THE PICTURESQUE TIBBS RUN PRESERVE, WEST VIRGINIA BOTANIC GARDEN IS HOME TO VERDANT AND BRIGHT VEGETATION AND BOTANICALS BY THE MILE.

THE BEAUTIFUL PLANT LIFE SURROUNDS AND REFLECTS OFF THE PROPERTY'S GLASSY POND AROUND WHICH TRAILS OF FLOWERING MEADOWS ENTWINE.

WEAVING IN AND OUT OF THE WOODLAND AND AROUND STREAMS, VISITORS LOVE TO STROLL, OBSERVE, AND CONTEMPLATE.

THE MORE THAN 80-ACRE RESERVE IS STILL DEVELOPING WHICH MEANS AS TIME GOES ON, THE ALREADY GORGEOUS LANDSCAPE OF WEST VIRGINIA BOTANIC GARDEN WILL ONLY GET BETTER.

ALTHOUGH VISITORS ARE WELCOME TO TOUR THE GROUNDS INDIVIDUALLY, GROUP-GUIDED TOURS ARE AVAILABLE UPON REQUEST.

IN ADDITION TO THE BOTANICALS YOU'LL SEE DURING YOUR TOUR, THE GARDEN ALSO HAS OTHER LOVELY FEATURES LIKE A FAIRY GARDEN, A WETLANDS BOARDWALK, A ROCK OUTCROPPING, AND A DAM.

FINALLY, WEST VIRGINIA ATTRACTIONS LIKE THIS ONE ARE A MUST DO FOR VISITORS TO THE STATE.

ADDRESS: 1061 TYRONE RD, MORGANTOWN, WV 26508, UNITED STATES

PASSPORT STAMPS:

NOTES :

The Greenbrier

VISTED DATE :   SPRING ◯ SUMMER ◯ FALL ◯ WINTER ◯

WEATHER :   ☀ ◯   ⛅ ◯   🌧 ◯   🌨 ◯   ⛈ ◯   🌬 ◯   🌡 TEMP :

FEE(S) :   RATING : ☆ ☆ ☆ ☆ ☆   WILL I RETURN?   YES / NO

LODGING :   WHO I WENT WITH :

DESCRIPTION / THINGS TO DO :

IF YOU'RE LOOKING FOR TOP-NOTCH VACATION IDEAS IN WEST VIRGINIA, LOOK NO FURTHER.

THIS MAGNIFICENT RESORT IS ONE OF THE MOST BEAUTIFUL TO VISIT IN WEST VIRGINIA.

SITUATED ON A VERDANT AND BEAUTIFULLY LANDSCAPED EXPANSE OF PROPERTY THAT ENCOMPASSES ACTIVITIES AND LUXURY FOR DAYS, THE GREENBRIER IS HOME TO MARVELOUS ACCOMMODATIONS LIKE COTTAGES AND HISTORICAL SUITES.

INCLUDED IN YOUR STAY ARE WORLD-CLASS AMENITIES LIKE OVERFLOWING WELCOME BASKETS, IN-ROOM HORS D'OEUVRES, COCKTAILS, AND MORE.

ESSENTIALLY, YOU'RE GIVEN THE ROYAL TREATMENT AS A GUEST OF THE RESORT. IN ADDITION TO THE LUXURIOUS ACCOMMODATIONS, THE RESORT HAS TONS OF FUN ACTIVITIES.

WITHIN THE HOTEL IS AN EPIC SPA, DINING OPTIONS FOR EVERY PALETTE, BOWLING, AN ARCADE, AN INDOOR POOL, AN ESCAPE ROOM, AND SO MUCH MORE.

OUTSIDE, THERE ARE EVEN MORE EXCITING ACTIVITIES LIKE A BEAUTIFUL POOL, GOLF, AN ADVENTURE COURSE, BIKE RENTALS, CANOPY TOURS, GEOCACHING, AND THE LIST GOES ON.

THE GREENBRIAR IS TRULY A RELIGIOUS EXPERIENCE AND ONE OF THE MANY WONDERFUL SITES TO SEE IN WEST VIRGINIA.

ADDRESS: 101 W MAIN ST, WHITE SULPHUR SPRINGS, WV 24986, UNITED STATES

PASSPORT STAMPS:

NOTES :

Heritage Farm Museum and Village

VISTED DATE :   SPRING ◯   SUMMER ◯   FALL ◯   WINTER ◯

WEATHER :   ☀ ◯   ⛅ ◯   🌧 ◯   🌨 ◯   ⛈ ◯   🌬 ◯   🌡 TEMP :

FEE(S) :   RATING : ☆ ☆ ☆ ☆ ☆   WILL I RETURN?   YES / NO

LODGING :   WHO I WENT WITH :

DESCRIPTION / THINGS TO DO :

IF YOU'RE INTERESTED IN FUN STUFF TO DO IN WEST VIRGINIA, HERITAGE FARM MUSEUM AND VILLAGE HAS SOMETHING FOR EVERYONE.

SITUATED UPON THE PROPERTY ARE 15 LOG STRUCTURES, ONE OF WHICH IS AN EVENT SPACE, WHILE THE OTHERS ARE LOG CABIN INNS, SEVEN OUTSTANDING MUSEUMS, AN ARTISAN CENTER, AND OTHER ATTRACTIONS.

ALTHOUGH LODGINGS ARE REMINISCENT OF PIONEER LIFE IN EARLY APPALACHIA, THEY ARE EQUIPPED WITH ALL THE BELLS AND WHISTLES.

WHETHER STAYING ON PROPERTY OR NOT, VISITORS HAVE SO MANY OPTIONS CONCERNING THINGS TO SEE AND WHAT TO DO.

SOME OF THE PROPERTY'S MOST BELOVED ATTRACTIONS INCLUDE VISITING UNIQUE PLACES LIKE MAKER SPACES, A BLACKSMITH SHOP, A LOG CHURCH, AN INTERACTIVE ANIMAL HABITAT, A NATURE CENTER, MANY ADVENTURE EXPERIENCES, AND MORE.

MOREOVER, THE SEVEN MUSEUMS RECOUNT THE HISTORY OF APPALACHIA THROUGH INTERESTINGLY THEMED DISPLAYS.

FINALLY, VACATIONS CAN BE HARD TO PLAN, BUT HERITAGE FARM MUSEUM AND VILLAGE IS A NO-BRAINER WITH SO MUCH TO DO IN ONE SPACE.

ADDRESS: 3300 HARVEY RD, HUNTINGTON, WV 25704, UNITED STATES

PASSPORT STAMPS:

NOTES :

Harpers Ferry

VISTED DATE :   SPRING ◯   SUMMER ◯   FALL ◯   WINTER ◯

WEATHER :   ☀ ◯   ⛅ ◯   🌧 ◯   🌨 ◯   ⛈ ◯   🌬 ◯   🌡 TEMP :

FEE(S) :   RATING : ☆ ☆ ☆ ☆ ☆   WILL I RETURN?   YES / NO

LODGING :   WHO I WENT WITH :

DESCRIPTION / THINGS TO DO :

THE QUAINT TOWN OF HARPERS FERRY IS SITUATED AMID THE NATIONAL PARK OF THE SAME NAME.

THIS HISTORIC WEST VIRGINIA VILLAGE IS A STEP BACK IN TIME.

THE PICTURESQUE STREETS OF THE VILLAGE SIT ALONG A STRETCH OF WATER WHERE THE SHENANDOAH AND POTOMAC RIVERS MEET, PROVIDING VIEWS OF MARYLAND AND VIRGINIA.

WHETHER VISITING TODAY OR THIS WEEKEND, HARPERS FERRY HAS SOMETHING FOR EVERYONE; THE TOWN IS HOME TO TOURIST ATTRACTIONS GALORE.

FOR INSTANCE, THE VILLAGE IS HOME TO INTERESTING EXHIBITS, MUSEUMS, HISTORIC BATTLEFIELDS, AND MORE.

FURTHERMORE, THERE ARE MANY FUN ACTIVITIES FOR CHILDREN, HIKING TRAILS (TRAILS RANGE FROM EASY TO DIFFICULT), CAMPING AREAS, ROCK CLIMBING, AND OTHER FUN OUTDOOR ADVENTURES.

ADDITIONALLY, THERE ARE MANY COOL HISTORICAL SIGHTS TO SEE LIKE JEFFERSON ROCK, A CHURCH BUILT IN THE 1800S, JOHN BROWN'S FORT, AND A HISTORIC TAVERN BUILT IN THE 1800S.

WITH SO MUCH BEAUTIFUL SCENERY AND AWESOME TOURIST ATTRACTIONS IN ONE PLACE, YOU WON'T BE DISAPPOINTED IN YOUR VISIT TO HARPERS FERRY.

ADDRESS: WV 25425, UNITED STATES

PASSPORT STAMPS:

NOTES :

Blackwater Falls State Park

VISTED DATE :   SPRING ◯   SUMMER ◯   FALL ◯   WINTER ◯

WEATHER :   ☀ ◯   ⛅ ◯   🌧 ◯   🌨 ◯   ⛈ ◯   💨 ◯   🌡 TEMP :

FEE(S) :   RATING : ☆ ☆ ☆ ☆ ☆   WILL I RETURN? YES / NO

LODGING :   WHO I WENT WITH :

DESCRIPTION / THINGS TO DO :

WEST VIRGINIA IS NOT SHORT ON TOURIST ATTRACTIONS WITH SPLENDID SCENERY.

ONE OF THE BEST PLACES TO VISIT IN WEST VIRGINIA, BLACKWATER FALLS STATE PARK IS SITUATED IN THE ALLEGHENY MOUNTAINS AND IS A FUN SIGHT TO SEE.

THE FALLS THEMSELVES ARE SO-NAMED FOR THE 57-FOOT CASCADE OF STUNNING AMBER WATERS.

ALONG WITH SOME OTHER EPIC SIGHTS WITHIN THE PARK, THE FALLS ARE ONE OF THE MOST PHOTOGRAPHED POINTS OF INTEREST IN WEST VIRGINIA.

THE FALLS CAN BE VISITED ALL YEAR LONG BY HIKING TO SCENIC OVERLOOKS OR VIEWING PLATFORMS SCATTERED THROUGHOUT THE PARK.

IN ADDITION TO THE MAGNIFICENT SCENERY, BLACKWATER FALLS STATE PARK HAS OVER 20 MILES OF HIKING TRAILS, AN AWESOME SLEDDING TRAIL ACCESSIBLE IN WINTER WEATHER, AND EVEN A COZY LODGE TO RELAX IN AFTER A LONG DAY OF ADVENTURE.

FINALLY, THE PARK ALSO HAS CAMPING AREAS THAT INCLUDE LOG CABINS, AS WELL AS MANY OTHER FUN OUTDOOR ADVENTURES.

OF OUTDOOR WEST VIRGINIA ATTRACTIONS, BLACKWATER FALLS STATE PARK IS A MUST-SEE PLACE.

ADDRESS: 1584 BLACKWATER LODGE RD, DAVIS, WV 26260, UNITED STATES

PASSPORT STAMPS:

NOTES :

West Virginia Penitentiary

VISTED DATE :   SPRING ◯   SUMMER ◯   FALL ◯   WINTER ◯

WEATHER : ☀️◯ ⛅◯ 🌧️◯ 🌨️◯ ⛈️◯ 🌬️◯   🌡️ TEMP :

FEE(S) :   RATING : ☆ ☆ ☆ ☆ ☆   WILL I RETURN?   YES / NO

LODGING :   WHO I WENT WITH :

DESCRIPTION / THINGS TO DO :

ONE OF THE MOST INTERESTING PLACES TO VISIT IN WEST VIRGINIA, THE STATE'S PENITENTIARY IS SURE TO LEAVE YOU CHILLED TO THE BONE.

SITUATED ON A 10-ACRE EXPANSE OF LAND, THE COLD AND GOTHIC BUILDING, WHICH WAS ERECTED IN THE LATE 1800S, WAS HOME TO THOUSANDS OF PRISONERS MORE THAN A HUNDRED OF WHICH WERE EXECUTED ON THE PREMISES.

ARCHITECTURALLY SPEAKING, WEST VIRGINIA PENITENTIARY IS A GOTHIC STONE BUILDING BEDECKED WITH TURRETS AND BATTLEMENTS.

THEMED TOURS ARE AVAILABLE TO THE PUBLIC THROUGHOUT THE YEAR. VISITORS MAY OPT FOR THE HISTORICAL DAY TOUR, A 90-MINUTE TOUR THAT SHARES THE PENITENTIARY'S HISTORY, LORE, ART, AND INSIGHT INTO THE CRIMINAL JUSTICE SYSTEM.

MOREOVER, THE MYSTERY MONDAY TOURS ARE A LITTLE MORE ACTION-PACKED WITH CLIMBING AND EXPLORING FEATURES.

FINALLY, THE ATTRACTION ALSO HOSTS GHOST HUNTS, SPOOKY NIGHT TOURS, AND AN ESCAPE FROM THE PRISON TOUR THAT'S LIKE AN ESCAPE ROOM BUT ON A LARGER SCALE.

ONE OF THE MOST UNIQUE POINTS OF INTEREST IN WV, THIS ATTRACTION IS HIGHLY RECOMMENDED.

ADDRESS: 818 JEFFERSON AVE, MOUNDSVILLE, WV 26041, UNITED STATES

PASSPORT STAMPS:

NOTES :

Greenbrier State Forest

VISTED DATE :   SPRING ◯ SUMMER ◯ FALL ◯ WINTER ◯

WEATHER : ☀ ◯ ⛅ ◯ 🌧 ◯ 🌨 ◯ ⛈ ◯ 🌬 ◯   🌡 TEMP :

FEE(S) :   RATING : ☆ ☆ ☆ ☆ ☆   WILL I RETURN?   YES / NO

LODGING :   WHO I WENT WITH :

DESCRIPTION / THINGS TO DO :

THE GREENBRIER STATE FOREST IS ONE OF THE MOST STUNNING WEST VIRGINIA ATTRACTIONS.

SITUATED ON MORE THAN 5,000 ACRES OF UNDEVELOPED FORESTRY, IT'S A WONDERFUL PLACE TO VISIT WITH FAMILY, FRIENDS, OR EVEN ALONE.

WITH MILES UPON MILES OF SECLUDED NATURAL BEAUTY LINED WITH HIKING TRAILS, BIKING TRAILS, AND MORE, THE FOREST PERMITS LOADS OF OTHER RECREATIONAL ATTRACTIONS LIKE FISHING AND SWIMMING.

BEST OF ALL, YOU COULD SPEND A NIGHT OR A FEW DAYS AT THE FOREST'S CAMPGROUNDS.

THIS FOREST SYSTEM IS MOST POPULAR FOR ITS HIKING TRAILS.

MOST NOTABLY, THE TRAILS RUN BETWEEN LEWISBURG AND WHITE SULPHUR SPRINGS, A DISTANCE OF MORE THAN FIVE MILES.

BESIDES COVERING A VAST DISTANCE, THE TRAILS WILL WEAVE YOU IN AND OUT OF SOME OF THE MOST BEAUTIFUL LANDSCAPES WEST VIRGINIA HAS TO OFFER.

ADDRESS: 1541 HARTS RUN RD, CALDWELL, WV 24925, UNITED STATES

PASSPORT STAMPS:

NOTES :

ACE Adventure Resort

VISTED DATE :   SPRING ◯   SUMMER ◯   FALL ◯   WINTER ◯

WEATHER :   ☀️◯   ⛅◯   🌧️◯   🌨️◯   ⛈️◯   🌬️◯   🌡️ TEMP :

FEE(S) :   RATING : ☆ ☆ ☆ ☆ ☆   WILL I RETURN?   YES / NO

LODGING :   WHO I WENT WITH :

DESCRIPTION / THINGS TO DO :

IF YOU'RE HEADING TO WEST VIRGINIA IN SEARCH OF HIGH-OCTANE ADVENTURE, THEN BE SURE TO BOOK AN APPOINTMENT WITH ACE ADVENTURE RESORT.

THIS ADVENTURE RESORT HAS ALL THE EXCITEMENT YOU NEED IN ONE CENTRAL LOCATION. THE RESORT'S PROPERTY HAS WONDERFUL ACCOMMODATIONS LIKE CLIFFSIDE CHALETS, LOG CABINS, AND TENT AND RV SITES FOR RENTAL.

THE RESORT IS HOME TO FIVE RESTAURANTS, THREE RETAIL LOCATIONS, AND EVEN FUN NIGHTLIFE. BUT BEST OF ALL, THE RESORT HAS TONS OF ADVENTUROUS ATTRACTIONS FOR VISITORS TO PARTAKE IN.

NOTABLY, THE RESORT'S BIGGEST ATTRACTION IS WHITEWATER RAFTING. THEY OFFER FULL-DAY, HALF-DAY, AND EVEN OVERNIGHT TRIPS ALONG DIFFERENT STRETCHES OF THE GAULEY RIVER.

BEYOND RAFTING THOUGH, THE RESORT ALSO HAS AN AWESOME WATERPARK, ZIPLINING, AN AERIAL PARK, A MUD OBSTACLE COURSE, ATV TOURS, AND MORE.

IN THE WATER, YOU CAN CANOE, KAYAK, SWIM, FISH, AND MORE. UNDOUBTEDLY, ACE ADVENTURE RESORT IS A ONE-STOP SHOP FOR ALL THE EXCITEMENT AND ADVENTURE YOU'RE LOOKING FOR.

ADDRESS: 1 CONCHO ROAD, OAK HILL, WV 25901, UNITED STATES

PASSPORT STAMPS:

NOTES :

Seneca Rocks

VISTED DATE :   SPRING ◯   SUMMER ◯   FALL ◯   WINTER ◯

WEATHER :   ☀ ◯   ⛅ ◯   🌧 ◯   🌨 ◯   ⛈ ◯   💨 ◯   🌡 TEMP :

FEE(S) :   RATING : ☆ ☆ ☆ ☆ ☆   WILL I RETURN?   YES / NO

LODGING :   WHO I WENT WITH :

DESCRIPTION / THINGS TO DO :

SENECA ROCKS, ONE OF MANY AWESOME WEST VIRGINIA ATTRACTIONS, IS ONE OF THE STATE'S MOST POPULAR NATURAL LANDMARKS.

OF NOTE, THE ROCKS ARE A SCENIC LOCALE THAT IS POPULAR WITH LOCALS AND TRAVELERS ALIKE.

BEYOND THE BEAUTIFUL BACKDROP FOR PHOTO OPPORTUNITIES, THE ROCKS SET THE STAGE FOR THRILL -SEEKERS TOO.

EACH YEAR, HUNDREDS OF ROCK CLIMBING ENTHUSIASTS TRAVEL TO SENECA ROCKS TO TRY THEIR LUCK AT THIS UNIQUE AND CHALLENGING ROCK FORMATION.

ASTOUNDINGLY, THE ROCKS CLIMB 900 FEET ABOVE THE PICTURESQUE NORTH FORK RIVER, ANOTHER BEAUTIFUL SIGHT TO SEE.

BESIDES ROCK CLIMBING, SENECA ROCKS IS ALSO A DESTINATION WITH LOTS OF OTHER WONDERFUL THINGS TO DO.

VISITORS CAN RIVER OR STREAM FISH, HIKE, OBSERVE NATURE/WILDLIFE, LEARN ABOUT THE AREA AT THE DISCOVERY CENTER, AND ENJOY AN ALFRESCO LUNCH AT THE PICNIC AREA. SENECA ROCKS IS ONE OF WEST VIRGINIA'S BEAUTIFUL NATURAL GEMS; BE SURE TO CHECK IT OUT DURING YOUR STAY IN THE STATE.

ADDRESS: WV 26884, UNITED STATES

PASSPORT STAMPS:

NOTES :

Seneca Caverns

VISTED DATE :   SPRING ◯   SUMMER ◯   FALL ◯   WINTER ◯

WEATHER : ☀️◯   ⛅◯   🌧️◯   🌨️◯   ⛈️◯   🌬️◯   🌡️ TEMP :

FEE(S) :   RATING : ☆ ☆ ☆ ☆ ☆   WILL I RETURN?   YES / NO

LODGING :   WHO I WENT WITH :

DESCRIPTION / THINGS TO DO :

IF YOU'RE LOOKING FOR ONE-OF-A-KIND THINGS TO DO IN WEST VIRGINIA, LOOK NO FURTHER. SENECA CAVERNS PROVIDES A UNIQUE HANDS-ON CAVERN EXPERIENCE.

REMARKABLY, THIS 450 MILLION-YEAR-OLD CAVERN IS FULL OF JAW-DROPPING FEATURES LIKE STALAGMITES, STALACTITES, FLOWSTONE, RIMSTONE POOLS, AND MORE.

THE SIGHTS YOU'LL SEE DURING A TOUR OF THE CAVERN ARE LIKE NOTHING YOU'LL EVER SEE ON LAND. CAVE TOURS ARE GUIDED, STUNNING, AND PROVIDE WONDERFUL PHOTO OPPORTUNITIES.

BEYOND SIMPLY TOURING THE CAVE VISITORS CAN ALSO PARTICIPATE IN GEMSTONE MINING.

YOU'LL HAVE SO MUCH FUN SIFTING THROUGH MUD, DIRT, AND SAND TO DISCOVER COOL MINERALS AND GEMS. BEST OF ALL, YOU CAN KEEP WHAT YOU FIND.

THIS IS AN AWESOME ACTIVITY FOR ADULTS AND CHILDREN ALIKE.

FINALLY, SENECA CAVERNS HAS A COOL GIFT SHOP, PICNIC AREAS, AND AN AWESOME RESTAURANT TOO.

SENECA FALLS IS A GREAT EXPERIENCE FOR ALL; BE SURE TO GIVE IT A TOP SPOT ON YOUR ITINERARY.

ADDRESS: 3328 GERMANY VALLEY RD, RIVERTON, WV 26814, UNITED STATES

PASSPORT STAMPS:

NOTES :

Lake Shawnee Amusement Park

VISTED DATE :   SPRING ◯   SUMMER ◯   FALL ◯   WINTER ◯

WEATHER :   ☀️◯   ⛅◯   🌧️◯   🌨️◯   ⛈️◯   🌬️◯   🌡️TEMP :

FEE(S) :   RATING : ☆ ☆ ☆ ☆ ☆   WILL I RETURN?   YES / NO

LODGING :   WHO I WENT WITH :

DESCRIPTION / THINGS TO DO :

IF YOU'RE IN THE MARKET FOR SOMETHING A BIT OFF THE BEATEN PATH, BE SURE TO VISIT LAKE SHAWNEE AMUSEMENT PARK.

THIS ABANDONED ATTRACTION IS SPOOKY AND UNSETTLING BUT AN ALTOGETHER FUN SIGHT TO SEE.

LOCAL LEGEND ASSERTS THAT THE PARK IS HAUNTED BY UNNATURAL SPIRITS, YET VISITORS COME FROM NEAR AND FAR NONETHELESS. SITUATED ON A NATIVE AMERICAN BURIAL GROUND AND THE SITE OF ALL TOO MANY VIOLENT DEATHS, THERE MAY BE SOMETHING TO THE IDEA THAT IT'S HAUNTED.

ABANDONED THOUGH IT IS, VISITORS CAN ARRANGE PRIVATE TOURS WITH GHOST HUNTERS TO DECIDE FOR THEMSELVES. IF YOU'RE INTO CREEPY, PARANORMAL, AND THE ALTOGETHER INEXPLICABLE, YOU'LL LOVE THIS ATTRACTION.

IN ADDITION TO MERELY TOURING THE PROPERTY, THE PARK ALSO HOSTS FUN SEASONAL EVENTS.

IF YOU HAPPEN TO BE IN WV IN OCTOBER, YOU WON'T WANT TO MISS THE "DARK CARNIVAL," WHEN YOU CAN HEAR PARK LEGENDS, HANG BY A CREEPY BONFIRE, PLAY WITH FREAKY CLOWNS, AND MORE.

YOU CAN EVEN CAMP OUT IN THE PARK IF YOU'RE BRAVE ENOUGH.

ADDRESS: 470 MATOAKA RD, ROCK, WV 24747, UNITED STATES

PASSPORT STAMPS:

NOTES :

Kruger Street Toy and Train Museum

VISTED DATE : SPRING ◯ SUMMER ◯ FALL ◯ WINTER ◯

WEATHER : ☀ ◯ ⛅ ◯ 🌧 ◯ 🌨 ◯ ⛈ ◯ 💨 ◯ 🌡 TEMP :

FEE(S) : RATING : ☆ ☆ ☆ ☆ ☆ WILL I RETURN? YES / NO

LODGING : WHO I WENT WITH :

DESCRIPTION / THINGS TO DO :

HOUSED IN THE BUILDING OF AN OLD ELEMENTARY SCHOOL, THE KRUGER STREET TOY AND TRAIN MUSEUM, BUILT IN 1906, IS SITUATED ON A HISTORIC SITE.

ONE OF THE MUSEUM'S QUIRKY BUT AFFABLE FEATURES IS THE RESIDENT CAT, LOO, WHO SAUNTERS ABOUT IN COSTUME AS IF HE OWNS THE PLACE.

THE MUSEUM'S BIGGEST COLLECTION AND DRAW THOUGH IS THE ASTONISHING TOY COLLECTION HOUSED THEREIN.

REMARKABLY, TOY EXHIBITS ARE ARRANGED THEMATICALLY AS FOLLOWS: TRANSPORTATION TOYS, MINIATURES, DOLLS, AND GAMES.

ENJOY THIS STEP BACK IN TIME WITH THE NOSTALGIC TOYS OF YOUR YOUTH. TRAIN-WISE, THE MUSEUM'S MOST POPULAR ATTRACTION IS A RESTORED CABOOSE THAT ONCE BELONGED ON THE B & O RAILROAD.

MOREOVER, THE MUSEUM HOUSES A TRAIN EXHIBIT THAT BOASTS LIONEL, AMERICAN FLYER, AND EVEN LAWRENCE LINER TRAINS.

FOR ADDED FUN, THE MUSEUM'S LOBBY DOUBLES AS A SMALL ARCADE. BE SURE TO HIT UP THE GIFT SHOP ON YOUR WAY FOR FUN NOVELTIES AND SOUVENIRS.

ADDRESS: 144 KRUGER ST, WHEELING, WV 26003, UNITED STATES

PASSPORT STAMPS:

NOTES:

Dolly Sods Wilderness Area

VISTED DATE :   SPRING ◯ SUMMER ◯ FALL ◯ WINTER ◯

WEATHER : ☀ ◯ 🌤 ◯ 🌧 ◯ 🌨 ◯ ⛈ ◯ 🌬 ◯   🌡 TEMP :

FEE(S) :   RATING : ☆ ☆ ☆ ☆ ☆   WILL I RETURN? YES / NO

LODGING :   WHO I WENT WITH :

DESCRIPTION / THINGS TO DO :

SPRAWLING ACROSS MORE THAN 17,000 ACRES OF FORESTRY, THE DOLLY SODS WILDERNESS IS AN EPIC NATURAL PRESERVATION THAT DRAWS VISITORS FROM FAR AND WIDE.

LOCATED ACROSS TWO WEST VIRGINIA COUNTIES, IT HAS A BLENDED ECO-TYPE, ELEVATIONS OF NEARLY 5,000 FEET, AND BEST OF ALL MANY WONDERFUL NATURAL FEATURES THAT SERVE AS A BACKDROP OF LOADS OF FUN RECREATION.

NOTABLY, DOLLY SODS IS HOME TO ALMOST 50 HIKING TRAILS SUITABLE FOR ALL EXPERIENCE LEVELS.

SOME OF THE TRAILS RUN ADJACENT TO OLD RAILROADS AND LOGGING ROADS MAKING FOR AN EVEN MORE SCENIC HIKE.

IN ADDITION TO LOADS OF HIKING TRAILS, VISITORS TO DOLLY SODS WILDERNESS AREA CAN ALSO FISH, SWIM, HUNT, AND HORSEBACK RIDE.

THROUGHOUT THE YEAR, YOU CAN EVEN PLAN A FEW DAYS AND NIGHTS AT THE AVAILABLE CAMPING GROUNDS. IN THE WINTER MONTHS, VISITORS MAY ALSO PARTAKE IN CROSS COUNTRY SKIING AND/OR SNOWSHOEING ON THE MANY TRAILS.

NO MATTER THE TIME OF YEAR, DOLLY SODS WILDERNESS AREA IS AN EXCELLENT WEST VIRGINIA ATTRACTION.

ADDRESS: WV, UNITED STATES

PASSPORT STAMPS:

NOTES :

Coopers Rock State Forest

VISTED DATE :   SPRING ◯ SUMMER ◯ FALL ◯ WINTER ◯

WEATHER : ☀️◯ ⛅◯ 🌧️◯ 🌨️◯ ⛈️◯ 🌬️◯   🌡️ TEMP :

FEE(S) :   RATING : ☆ ☆ ☆ ☆ ☆   WILL I RETURN? YES / NO

LODGING :   WHO I WENT WITH :

DESCRIPTION / THINGS TO DO :

FOUNDED IN 1936 THIS ASTONISHING PARK BOASTS SOME OF THE MOST GLORIOUS SIGHTS IN ALL OF WEST VIRGINIA.

SERENELY SITUATED AMID THE APTLY NAMED TOWN OF ALMOST HEAVEN, COOPERS ROCK STATE FOREST IS A FAVORITE OF LOCALS.

SOME OF THE PARK'S MANY STUNNING FEATURES INCLUDE CANYON OVERLOOKS, HISTORICAL AREAS, AND MORE THAN 50 MILES OF HIKING AND BIKING TRAILS.

OTHER NATURAL FEATURES INCLUDE SANDSTONE CLIFFS AND EPIC BOULDERS FOR ROCK CLIMBING, TERRAIN SUITABLE FOR CROSS COUNTRY SKIING, AND MORE.

IN ADDITION TO THESE LAND FEATURES, THERE'S ALSO A CENTRAL LAKE THAT VISITORS LOVE TO USE FOR FISHING, SWIMMING, RAFTING, AND OTHER WATER SPORTS.

OTHER OUTDOOR ADVENTURES AT COOPERS ROCK STATE FOREST INCLUDE GOLFING, HUNTING, AND GEOCACHING. WHILE VISITING THE PARK, VISITORS LOVE TO ENJOY ALFRESCO MEALS IN THE LOVELY PICNIC PAVILIONS.

FINALLY, IF YOU PREFER TO STAY IN THE PARK FOR AN EXTENDED PERIOD, THERE ARE CAMPING ACCOMMODATIONS AS WELL AS CONVENIENT PRE-SET CANVAS TENT SITES.

ADDRESS: 61 COUNTY LINE DR, BRUCETON MILLS, WV 26525, UNITED STATES

PASSPORT STAMPS:

NOTES:

Appalachian National Scenic Trail

VISTED DATE :   SPRING ◯   SUMMER ◯   FALL ◯   WINTER ◯

WEATHER :   ☀️◯   ⛅◯   🌧️◯   🌨️◯   ⛈️◯   🌬️◯   🌡️TEMP :

FEE(S) :   RATING : ☆ ☆ ☆ ☆ ☆   WILL I RETURN?   YES / NO

LODGING :   WHO I WENT WITH :

DESCRIPTION / THINGS TO DO :

THIS FAMOUS AMERICAN TRAIL IS A RITE OF PASSAGE FOR OUTDOOR ENTHUSIASTS, SO IF YOU'RE PLANNING A TRIP TO WEST VIRGINIA BE SURE TO BOOKMARK TIME TO CHECK IT OUT.

THE APPALACHIAN NATIONAL SCENIC TRAIL CONSISTS OF MORE THAN 2,000 MILES OF FOOTPATH.

THE TRAIL IS SCENIC, SERENE, PASTORAL, AND ALTOGETHER AMAZING.

BUILT BY PRIVATE CITIZENS AND OPENED IN 1937, THE TRAIL HAS BEEN A NATIONAL ATTRACTION SINCE.

NOTABLY, THE TRAIL RUNS THROUGH 14 US STATES, BEGINNING IN GEORGIA (DEPENDING ON WHERE YOU BEGIN), PASSING THROUGH WEST VIRGINIA, AND ENDING IN MAINE.

ALTHOUGH THE WV LEG OF THE TRAIL IS SHORT, IT IS THE MOST POPULAR.

ALONG THE WV LEG OF THE TRAIL, HIKERS PASS THROUGH HARPERS FERRY NATIONAL HISTORICAL PARK, THE CAMPUS OF STORER COLLEGE, AND OTHER HISTORIC LANDMARKS.

SIGNIFICANTLY, THE WV PORTION OF THE TRAIL IS CONSIDERED ITS HALFWAY POINT, AND IT'S ALSO WHERE YOU'LL FIND THE APPALACHIAN TRAIL CONSERVANCY, A POPULAR RESTING POINT.

ADDRESS: HARPERS FERRY, WV 25425, UNITED STATES

PASSPORT STAMPS:

NOTES:

Arthurdale Historic District

VISTED DATE :   SPRING ◯   SUMMER ◯   FALL ◯   WINTER ◯

WEATHER :   ☀️◯   ⛅◯   🌧️◯   🌨️◯   ⛈️◯   🌬️◯   🌡️ TEMP :

FEE(S) :   RATING : ☆ ☆ ☆ ☆ ☆   WILL I RETURN?   YES / NO

LODGING :   WHO I WENT WITH :

DESCRIPTION / THINGS TO DO :

ESTABLISHED IN 1933 THROUGH PRESIDENT ROOSEVELT'S NEW DEAL LEGISLATION, THE COMMUNITY OF ARTHURDALE PROVIDED A FRESH START TO WV RESIDENTS WHO SUFFERED DURING THE GREAT DEPRESSION.

HISTORICALLY, FIRST LADY ELEANOR ROOSEVELT WAS THE TOWN'S BENEFACTRESS AND THE TOWN BECAME COLLOQUIALLY KNOWN AS "ELEANOR'S LITTLE VILLAGE."

TODAY, THE SAME CHARM THAT EXISTED NEARLY 90 YEARS AGO REMAINS. THE TOWN REMAINS VIRTUALLY UNTOUCHED BY MODERNITY WHILE REMAINING OPEN FOR HISTORIC TOURS.

DURING A TOUR OF THE AREA, VISITORS CAN LEARN ABOUT THE TOWN'S RICH HERITAGE, VIEW PHOTO GALLERIES, HEAR LOCAL STORIES, VISIT SHOPS, AND MORE.

THE DISTRICT'S CENTRAL FEATURE IS THE NEW DEAL HOMESTEAD MUSEUM WHICH IS FILLED WITH ARTIFACTS FROM THE TOWN'S EARLY BEGINNINGS.

ONE OF THE MUSEUM'S MOST POPULAR EXHIBITS IS THE CRAFT SHOP WHICH DISPLAYS AND SELLS CRAFTS MADE BY LOCAL ARTISTS.

IF YOU'VE GOT SPACE ON YOUR ITINERARY, BE SURE TO SCHEDULE A TOUR OF THIS HISTORY-RICH WEST VIRGINIA LOCALE.

ADDRESS: 13272 N MOUNTAINEER HWY, REEDSVILLE, WV 26547, UNITED STATES

PASSPORT STAMPS:

NOTES:

Mountwood Park

VISTED DATE :   SPRING ◯   SUMMER ◯   FALL ◯   WINTER ◯

WEATHER :   ☀️◯ ⛅◯ 🌧️◯ 🌨️◯ ⛈️◯ 💨◯   🌡️ TEMP :

FEE(S) :   RATING : ☆ ☆ ☆ ☆ ☆   WILL I RETURN?   YES / NO

LODGING :   WHO I WENT WITH :

DESCRIPTION / THINGS TO DO :

THIS AMAZING PARK IS A BEAUTIFUL SITE FOR ALL THINGS OUTDOORS INCLUDING EPIC CAMPING.

AT MOUNTWOOD PARK, GUESTS CAN RENT LAKESIDE CAMPSITES, A LAKE HOUSE, AND CABINS EACH OF WHICH IS EQUIPPED WITH MANY CONVENIENT AMENITIES.

ALTHOUGH THE BEAUTIFUL PARK BACKDROP OF THE CAMPSITES IS A WONDERFUL DRAW FOR GUESTS, THE BIGGER DRAW IS ALL OF THE AWESOME RECREATION OPPORTUNITIES.

SITUATED ON A 50-ACRE LAKE AND SURROUNDED BY MORE THAN 50 MILES OF HIKING TRAILS, THE OPPORTUNITIES FOR ACTION-PACKED FUN ARE ENDLESS.

OF NOTE, THE PARK IS HOME TO GORGEOUS WOODED PICNIC AREAS, AN ARCHERY RANGE, BIRDWATCHING, DISC GOLF, A DOG PARK, FISHING AND BOATING, AND BEYOND.

ADDITIONALLY, THE PARK IS HOME TO A LEGENDARY ATV PARK WHERE VISITORS RIP AROUND THE 600 ACRES OF TRAILS ON DIRTBIKES AND QUADS.

MOREOVER, A PARK MUSEUM SITS AT THE CENTER OF THE PARK HOUSING HISTORICAL ARTIFACTS ASSOCIATED WITH THE PARK.

ADDRESS: 1014 VOLCANO RD, WAVERLY, WV 26184, UNITED STATES

PASSPORT STAMPS:

NOTES :

Tygart Lake State Park

VISTED DATE :   SPRING ◯   SUMMER ◯   FALL ◯   WINTER ◯

WEATHER :   ☀ ◯   ⛅ ◯   🌧 ◯   🌨 ◯   ⛈ ◯   🌬 ◯   🌡 TEMP :

FEE(S) :   RATING : ☆ ☆ ☆ ☆ ☆   WILL I RETURN?   YES / NO

LODGING :   WHO I WENT WITH :

DESCRIPTION / THINGS TO DO :

TYGART LAKE STATE PARK MAY BE ONE OF THE MOST STUNNING TRACTS IN ALL OF WEST VIRGINIA.

BEAUTIFULLY, THE PARK SITS UPON THE 10-MILE LONG AND 1,750-ACRE BREATHTAKING LAKE WHICH VISITORS OGLE AT.

NOTABLY, THE PARK HAS CAMPING ACCOMMODATIONS AS WELL AS THE EVER-POPULAR 20-ROOM LODGE. THE LODGE SITS UPON AN ELEVATED PENINSULA OVERLOOKING THE SHIMMERING LAKE.

THE LODGE HAS A DELICIOUS FULL-SERVICE RESTAURANT, A MARINA, AND A NATURE CENTER. THE EXTRAORDINARY LAKE SERVES AS THE TEMPLATE FOR TONS OF ADVENTUROUS RECREATION.

UPON THE PARK'S PROPERTY, RECREATIONAL ACTIVITIES INCLUDE GEOCACHING, SWIMMING, BOATING, HIKING, AND FISHING.

THE AFOREMENTIONED LODGE PROVIDES KAYAK AND CANOE RENTALS FOR GUESTS. OFF PROPERTY, JUST A STONE'S THROW AWAY, VISITORS CAN BIKE, GOLF, AND HUNT.

FINALLY, THE LAKE'S EPIC INFLATABLE LAKE PARK IS AN EXCITING WAY TO SPEND THE DAY FOR BOTH CHILDREN AND ADULTS. NO MATTER THE SEASON DURING WHICH YOU'LL VISIT, TYGART LAKE STATE PARK IS A GREAT TIME WAITING TO BE HAD.

ADDRESS: 1240 PAUL E MALONE RD, GRAFTON, WV 26354, UNITED STATES

PASSPORT STAMPS:

NOTES :

Trans-Allegheny Lunatic Asylum

VISTED DATE : SPRING ○ SUMMER ○ FALL ○ WINTER ○

WEATHER : ☀ ○ ⛅ ○ 🌧 ○ 🌨 ○ ⛈ ○ 🌬 ○   🌡 TEMP :

FEE(S) : RATING : ☆ ☆ ☆ ☆ ☆   WILL I RETURN? YES / NO

LODGING : WHO I WENT WITH :

DESCRIPTION / THINGS TO DO :

THIS NATIONAL HISTORIC SITE IS BOTH MYSTERIOUS AND INTERESTING.

FORMERLY KNOWN AS THE WESTON STATE HOSPITAL, THE TRANS-ALLEGHENY LUNATIC ASYLUM BEGAN SERVING THE MENTALLY ILL IN THE MID-1800S.

HOWEVER, MORE THAN THAT, THE ASYLUM HAS BEEN THE SITE OF MANY HISTORICAL EVENTS LIKE A CIVIL WAR RAID AND A GOLD ROBBERY.

TODAY THE ASYLUM HOSTS BOTH HISTORICAL TOURS AND PARANORMAL TOURS. THE ASYLUM'S HERITAGE TOURS EXPLORE PIONEERING METHODS IN THE HUMANE TREATMENT OF THE MENTALLY ILL, A PEEK AT PATIENT WARDS, THE MEDICAL SUITE, AND A GERIATRIC BUILDING.

IF YOU'RE LOOKING FOR SOMETHING A LITTLE MORE THRILLING, THE ASYLUM'S GHOST TOURS ARE AN INTERESTING ATTRACTION. SOME BELIEVE THE DECOMMISSIONED ASYLUM IS HAUNTED; ARE YOU BRAVE ENOUGH TO DECIDE FOR YOURSELF?

VISITORS HAVE REPORTED STRANGE SIGHTINGS, SPOOKY NOISES, AND ALTOGETHER CREEPY OCCURRENCES. DURING AN ASYLUM GHOST TOUR VISITORS STEP BACK IN TIME TO SEE HOW PATIENTS LIVED AND DIED (AND MAY CONTINUE TO LIVE ON IN SPIRIT).

BY THE END OF A GHOST TOUR, YOU'LL HAVE TO DECIDE FOR YOURSELF IF THE PROPERTY IS TRULY HAUNTED.

ADDRESS: 50 S RIVER AVE, WESTON, WV 26452, UNITED STATES

PASSPORT STAMPS:

NOTES :

Oglebay Resort

VISTED DATE :   SPRING ◯ SUMMER ◯ FALL ◯ WINTER ◯

WEATHER :   ☀️◯ 🌤️◯ 🌧️◯ 🌨️◯ ⛈️◯ 💨◯   🌡️TEMP :

FEE(S) :   RATING : ☆ ☆ ☆ ☆ ☆   WILL I RETURN?   YES / NO

LODGING :   WHO I WENT WITH :

DESCRIPTION / THINGS TO DO :

THIS AWESOME WEST VIRGINIA RESORT IS HOME TO LUXURY, RELAXATION, AND EXCELLENT RECREATIONAL ACTIVITIES.

OGLEBAY RESORT, LOCATED IN WHEELING, WV, IS A PICTURESQUE BACKDROP TO A VERDANT GOLF COURSE, HORSEBACK RIDING, HIKING, A GORGEOUS LAKE, AN AERIAL OBSTACLE COURSE, AND MORE.

ALSO HOUSED AT THE RESORT IS THE EXTRAORDINARY WHEELING PARK WHICH HAS AN OLYMPIC-SIZED POOL, TENNIS COURTS, A WATERPARK, AND EVEN AN ICE SKATING RINK.

IN ADDITION TO ALL OF THE RECREATIONAL OPPORTUNITIES AT OGLEBAY RESORT, THERE ARE MANY RELAXING FEATURES TOO.

THE WEST SPA PROVIDES LUXURIOUS SPA SERVICES IN THE 5,000 SQUARE FOOT FACILITY. MOREOVER, THERE ARE 10 ON-SITE RESTAURANTS SPECIALIZING IN AN ARRAY OF CUISINES.

ON TOP OF ALL OF THIS, THE RESORT IS ALSO HOME TO THE GOOD ZOO WHICH CARES FOR MORE THAN 50 SPECIES OF ANIMALS LIKE HOGS, BOBCATS, PANDAS, CHEETAHS, LEOPARDS, AND MORE.

REMARKABLY, THE OGLEBAY RESORT IS A ONE-STOP VACATION DESTINATION THAT HAS TONS TO DO IN ONE CENTRAL LOCATION.

ADDRESS: 465 LODGE DR, WHEELING, WV 26003, UNITED STATES

PASSPORT STAMPS:

NOTES :

Mountaineer Field

VISTED DATE : SPRING ○ SUMMER ○ FALL ○ WINTER ○

WEATHER : ☀ ○ ⛅ ○ ☁ ○ 🌨 ○ ⛈ ○ 🌬 ○   🌡 TEMP :

FEE(S) :   RATING : ☆ ☆ ☆ ☆ ☆   WILL I RETURN? YES / NO

LODGING :   WHO I WENT WITH :

DESCRIPTION / THINGS TO DO :

WEST VIRGINIA UNIVERSITY'S MOUNTAINEER FIELD AT MILAN PUSKAR STADIUM IS THE HIGH-ENERGY HOME OF THE MOUNTAINEERS FOOTBALL TEAM. ONCE FOOTBALL SEASON GETS UNDERWAY IN THE FALL, MOUNTAINEER FIELD IS THE PLACE TO BE.

BEFORE FANS ENTER THE STADIUM, THE TAILGATE GAME IS LIKE NONE OTHER. BUT AS FANS ENTER THE STADIUM, WHICH CAN SEAT 60,000 FANS, IT ERUPTS WITH EXCITEMENT WHEN THE TEAM TAKES THE FIELD.

CHEERLEADERS GET THE CROWD GOING WITH WORLD-CLASS ROUTINES AND THE ELECTRICITY THAT TRAVELS THROUGH THE STANDS IS PALPABLE.

AT KICKOFF, THE REAL ENTHUSIASM KICKS INTO HIGH GEAR AND DOESN'T RELENT UNTIL THE FINAL WHISTLE.

IN ADDITION TO THE ACTION OF THE AWESOME GAMES, THE STADIUM IS ALSO RICH IN HISTORY. AS VISITORS STROLL THROUGH THE CORRIDORS THEY ARE TREATED TO A HISTORY OF PLAYERS, GAMES, AND STORIES OF YESTERYEAR.

WHETHER YOU'RE A COLLEGE FOOTBALL FAN OR NOT, THE GOOD TIMES AND HISTORY ARE WORTH A VISIT TO MOUNTAINEER FIELD.

ADDRESS: 1 IRA ERRETT RODGERS DR, MORGANTOWN, WV 26505, UNITED STATES

PASSPORT STAMPS:

NOTES :

Clay Center for the Arts and Sciences

VISTED DATE :   SPRING ◯   SUMMER ◯   FALL ◯   WINTER ◯

WEATHER :   ☀ ◯   ⛅ ◯   🌧 ◯   🌨 ◯   ⛈ ◯   🌬 ◯   🌡 TEMP :

FEE(S) :   RATING : ☆ ☆ ☆ ☆ ☆   WILL I RETURN?   YES / NO

LODGING :   WHO I WENT WITH :

DESCRIPTION / THINGS TO DO :

CLAY CENTER FOR THE ARTS AND SCIENCES WAS ESTABLISHED IN 2003 AS A FORERUNNING ARTS CENTER.

THE NEARLY 250,000 SQUARE FOOT CENTER IS HOME TO PERFORMING ARTS PRODUCTIONS, VISUAL ARTS EXHIBITS AND EDUCATION, AND SCIENCE PROGRAMS.

THE CENTER'S VISION IS TO ADVANCE AND INSPIRE CREATIVITY, DISCOVERY, AND LEARNING THROUGH ARTS AND SCIENCE.

SITUATED IN THE WV CAPITAL OF CHARLESTON, THE CENTER HOUSES A DISCOVERY MUSEUM, AN ART MUSEUM, AND A PERFORMANCE THEATRE.

THE JULIET ART MUSEUM ACCOMMODATES TRAVELING EXHIBITS FROM ALL OVER THE COUNTRY AS WELL AS ART FROM AN ASTOUNDING PERMANENT COLLECTION.

AVAMPATO DISCOVERY MUSEUM IS THREE FLOORS OF HANDS-ON ACTIVITIES SUITABLE FOR INQUISITIVE CHILDREN.

FINALLY, THIS IS A SUPERB ATTRACTION TO VISIT IF YOU HAPPEN TO BE IN THE STATE'S ILLUSTRIOUS CAPITAL.

ADDRESS: 1 CLAY SQUARE, CHARLESTON, WV 25301, UNITED STATES

PASSPORT STAMPS:

NOTES :

Grand Vue Park

VISTED DATE :   SPRING ◯ SUMMER ◯ FALL ◯ WINTER ◯

WEATHER :   ☀️◯ 🌤️◯ 🌧️◯ 🌨️◯ ⛈️◯ 💨◯   🌡️TEMP :

FEE(S) :   RATING : ☆ ☆ ☆ ☆ ☆   WILL I RETURN?   YES / NO

LODGING :   WHO I WENT WITH :

DESCRIPTION / THINGS TO DO :

GRAND VUE PARK IS A 650-ACRE OUTDOOR HAVEN THAT PROVIDES ADVENTUROUS TRAVELERS WITH A MENU OF OUTDOOR ACTIVITIES.

THRILL-SEEKERS ARE IN FOR A TREAT WITH THEIR ZIPLINE CANOPY TOUR, FEATURING EIGHT DUAL ZIPLINES AND THREE SUSPENSION BRIDGES AS WELL AS A HIGH-FLYING ZIPLINE 2,100 FEET ABOVE THE GROUND THAT WHIPS THROUGH THE TREES TO OFFER ASTOUNDING VIEWS OF DOWNTOWN - MOUNDSVILLE.

THE AERIAL ADVENTURE PARK FEATURES A 40-FOOT ROPE COURSE WITH RAPPELLING AND FREEFALL DROP ZONES, BUNGEE TRAMPOLINES, AND A 28-FOOT ROCK WALL.

GUESTS CAN ALSO HIKE OR BIKE 12 MILES OF NATURE TRAILS, PLAY DISK GOLF, HANG OUT AT THE POOL AND SPLASHGROUND, AND PLAY PAINTBALL, AMONG OTHER ACTIVITIES.

ADDRESS: 250 TRAIL DRIVE, MOUNDSVILLE, WV, UNITED STATES

PASSPORT STAMPS:

NOTES :

Audra State Park

VISTED DATE :   SPRING ○   SUMMER ○   FALL ○   WINTER ○

WEATHER :   ☀ ○   ⛅ ○   🌧 ○   🌨 ○   ⛈ ○   🌬 ○   TEMP :

FEE(S) :   RATING : ☆ ☆ ☆ ☆ ☆   WILL I RETURN?   YES / NO

LODGING :   WHO I WENT WITH :

DESCRIPTION / THINGS TO DO :

THOSE LOOKING TO ESCAPE THE HUSTLE AND BUSTLE OF CITY LIFE CAN GET AWAY FROM IT ALL BY SPENDING SOME TIME AT AUDRA STATE PARK.

SITUATED IN SOUTHWESTERN BARBOUR COUNTY AND COVERING PARTS OF UPSHUR COUNTY, WEST VIRGINIA, AUDRA STATE PARK SURROUNDS VISITORS WITH WOODLANDS AND NATURAL BEAUTY.

CRISP, CLEAN WATER FLOWS DOWN THE MIDDLE FORK RIVER, A TRIBUTARY OF THE TYGART VALLEY RIVER.

HIKERS CAN EXPLORE THE ROCK CLIFF OF THE ALUM CAVE. A DAY AT AUDRA MEANS AMPLE OPPORTUNITY FOR OUTDOORS ACTIVITIES LIKE HIKING AND FAMILY PICNICS.

THE PARK ALSO ALLOWS CAMPERS TO STAY OVERNIGHT AND SLEEP UNDERNEATH THE STARS.

ADDRESS: 8397 AUDRA PARK ROAD, BUCKHANNON, WV, UNITED STATES

PASSPORT STAMPS:

NOTES :

Babcock State Park

VISTED DATE :   SPRING ○ SUMMER ○ FALL ○ WINTER ○

WEATHER :   ☀ ○ ⛅ ○ ☁ ○ 🌧 ○ ⛈ ○ 🌬 ○   🌡 TEMP :

FEE(S) :   RATING : ☆ ☆ ☆ ☆ ☆   WILL I RETURN?   YES / NO

LODGING :   WHO I WENT WITH :

DESCRIPTION / THINGS TO DO :

NESTLED IN CLIFFTOP, WEST VIRGINIA, BABCOCK STATE PARK SPANS 4,127 ACRES.

THE ATTRACTION HAS NO SHORTAGE OF OUTDOOR ACTIVITIES, ESPECIALLY FOR THE ADVENTUROUS.

THRILL-SEEKERS CAN SPEND THE DAY WHITEWATER RAFTING AND ZIP LINING.

BABCOCK STATE PARK HAS 13 CABINS ALONG GLADE CREEK AVAILABLE FOR RENT WHICH COME FULLY-EQUIPPED WITH A KITCHEN, SHOWER, AND BATHROOM.

GUESTS CAN ALSO SET UP TENTS, RVS, OR CAMPERS AT THE 52-UNIT CAMPGROUND. OUTDOORSMEN CAN ENJOY A DAY OF FISHING OR HUNTING.

TRAILS GIVE HIKERS A CHANCE TO EXPLORE THE PARK, VIEW WILDLIFE, AND TAKE IN THE FRESH AIR.

THE PARK ALSO HAS TWO GEOCACHE SITES FOR SCAVENGER HUNTING ADVENTURES.

ADDRESS: 486 BABCOCK ROAD, CLIFFTOP, WV, UNITED STATES

PASSPORT STAMPS:

NOTES :

Beartown State Park

VISTED DATE :　　　　　　　SPRING ○　SUMMER ○　FALL ○　WINTER ○

WEATHER :　☀ ○　⛅ ○　🌧 ○　🌨 ○　⛈ ○　🌬 ○　🌡 TEMP :

FEE(S) :　　　　RATING : ☆ ☆ ☆ ☆ ☆　　WILL I RETURN?　YES / NO

LODGING :　　　　　　　WHO I WENT WITH :

DESCRIPTION / THINGS TO DO :

BEARTOWN STATE PARK SITS BELOW THE EASTERN SUMMIT OF DROOP MOUNTAIN IN WEST VIRGINIA'S GREENBRIER AND POCAHONTAS COUNTIES.

GUESTS COME TO EXPLORE THE UNIQUE ROCK FORMATIONS, CAVES, AND BOULDERS.

JUTTING CLIFFS GIVE PICTURESQUE VIEWS OF THE SURROUNDING LANDSCAPE.

THE HALF-MILE LONG BOARDWALK PROVIDES AN EASY STROLL WHILE ENJOYING THE PARK'S NATURAL BEAUTY.

BEARTOWN ALSO OFFERS GEOCACHING ACTIVITIES FOR FAMILIES AND NATURE-LOVERS TO SPEND TIME SCAVENGER HUNTING OUTDOORS.

ALTHOUGH THE PARK REMAINS OPEN FOR DAY-USE ONLY, VISITORS CAN CAMP OUT OR RENT CABINS AT THE SENECA STATE FOREST OR WATOGA STATE PARK.

THE CIVIL WAR'S LAST MAJOR BATTLE SITE, DROOP MOUNTAIN, IS ALSO NEARBY.

ADDRESS: BEARTOWN ROAD, RENICK, WV, UNITED STATES

PASSPORT STAMPS:

NOTES :

Berkeley Springs State Park

VISTED DATE :   SPRING ◯ SUMMER ◯ FALL ◯ WINTER ◯

WEATHER : ☀️◯ ⛅◯ 🌧️◯ 🌨️◯ ⛈️◯ 🌬️◯   🌡️ TEMP :

FEE(S) :   RATING : ☆ ☆ ☆ ☆ ☆   WILL I RETURN? YES / NO

LODGING :   WHO I WENT WITH :

DESCRIPTION / THINGS TO DO :

SINCE THE COLONIAL PERIOD, RESIDENTS OF THE AREA VISITED BERKELEY SPRINGS TO BENEFIT FROM ITS NATURAL, HOT MINERAL SPRINGS.

WARM SPRING WATER STAYS AT AN AVERAGE TEMPERATURE OF 74 DEGREES FAHRENHEIT.

TODAY, BERKELEY SPRINGS STATE PARK HOSTS A RANGE OF SPA ACTIVITIES. GUESTS CAN ENJOY THE NATURAL SURROUNDINGS IN BETWEEN GETTING A MESSAGE, VISITING THE SAUNAS, OR RELAXING IN A ROMAN BATHHOUSE.

THE BATHHOUSE HAS A FREE MUSEUM ON THE SECOND FLOOR FEATURING DISPLAYS OF HISTORICAL ARTIFACTS.

BERKELEY SPRINGS ALSO HAS A SWIMMING POOL FILLED ENTIRELY WITH NATURAL SPRING WATER.

NEARBY, GOLFERS CAN TEE OFF AT THE CACAPON RESORT STATE PARK'S CHAMPIONSHIP COURSE.

ADDRESS: 2 SOUTH WASHINGTON STREET, BERKELEY SPRINGS, WV, UNITED STATES

PASSPORT STAMPS:

NOTES :

Bluestone State Park

VISTED DATE :   SPRING ○   SUMMER ○   FALL ○   WINTER ○

WEATHER : ☀ ○   ⛅ ○   🌧 ○   🌨 ○   ⛈ ○   🌬 ○   🌡 TEMP :

FEE(S) :   RATING : ☆ ☆ ☆ ☆ ☆   WILL I RETURN?   YES / NO

LODGING :   WHO I WENT WITH :

DESCRIPTION / THINGS TO DO :

LOCATED IN HINTON, WEST VIRGINIA, BLUESTONE STATE PARK PROVIDES A LAKESIDE GETAWAY WITH BREATHTAKING VIEWS OF THE WILDERNESS.

AS THE STATE'S LARGEST PARK, BLUESTONE OFFERS IT ALL FOR NATURE LOVERS. RECREATIONAL ACTIVITIES IN THE LAKE INCLUDE BOATING, FISHING, AND SWIMMING.

ADRENALINE JUNKIES CAN OPT FOR MORE ADVENTUROUS OPTIONS LIKE ROCK CLIMBING, WHITE WATER RAFTING, AERIAL TOURS, AND MOUNTAIN BIKING.

BLUESTONE WELCOMES GUESTS TO STAY OVERNIGHT AT ONE OF FOUR CAMPGROUNDS. 32 OF THE SITES ACCOMMODATE RVS AND TENTS WITH ELECTRIC AND WATER HOOKUPS AVAILABLE AND A CENTRAL BATHHOUSE.

GOLFERS CAN TEE OFF AT ONE OF TWO COURSES AT THE NEARBY PIPESTEM RESORT STATE PARK.

ADDRESS: 78 HC, HINTON, WV, UNITED STATES

PASSPORT STAMPS:

NOTES :

Cacapon Resort State Park

VISTED DATE :   SPRING ◯   SUMMER ◯   FALL ◯   WINTER ◯

WEATHER : ☀️◯   🌤️◯   🌧️◯   🌨️◯   ⛈️◯   🌬️◯   🌡️TEMP :

FEE(S) :   RATING : ☆ ☆ ☆ ☆ ☆   WILL I RETURN?   YES / NO

LODGING :   WHO I WENT WITH :

DESCRIPTION / THINGS TO DO :

CACAPON RESORT STATE PARK COVERS 6,000 ACRES OF WOODLANDS OFFERING NATURE LOVERS A CHANCE TO ESCAPE TO THE GREAT OUTDOORS.

THE HIGHEST PEAK IN EASTERN WEST VIRGINIA OVERLOOKS THE PARK.

THE ADJACENT LAKE PROVIDES AMPLE WATER ACTIVITIES, FROM DAYTIME TROUT FISHING TO OVERNIGHT FISHING TRIPS.

SPORTSMEN COME TO HUNT FOR DEER, TURKEY, SQUIRREL, AND GROUSE.

GEOCACHING GIVE GUESTS A CHANCE TO EXPLORE THE PARK IN SEARCH OF BURIED TREASURE.

THE RESORT ORGANIZES HORSEBACK AND PONY RIDING OUT ON THE TRAILS.

MOUNTAIN BIKERS OF ALL LEVELS CAN GET THEIR THRILLS ON VARIED TERRAINS WITH EXPANSIVE WILDERNESS VIEWS.

ADDRESS: 818 CACAPON LODGE DRIVE, BERKELEY SPRINGS, WV, UNITED STATES

PASSPORT STAMPS:

NOTES :

Cass Scenic Railroad State Park

VISTED DATE :   SPRING ◯   SUMMER ◯   FALL ◯   WINTER ◯

WEATHER : ☀ ◯ ⛅ ◯ 🌧 ◯ 🌨 ◯ ⛈ ◯ 🌬 ◯   🌡 TEMP :

FEE(S) :   RATING : ☆ ☆ ☆ ☆ ☆   WILL I RETURN? YES / NO

LODGING :   WHO I WENT WITH :

DESCRIPTION / THINGS TO DO :

CASS SCENIC RAILROAD STATE PARK TRANSPORTS VISITORS BACK TO A TIME WHEN PEOPLE RELIED ON STEAM-DRIVEN LOCOMOTIVES TO GET AROUND.

RAILROAD ENTHUSIASTS AND HISTORY BUFFS WILL LOVE THE REMAINING 11-MILE RAILROAD TRACK AND PRESERVED LUMBERING TOWN OF CASS.

IT'S ALL ABOARD, AND VISITORS CAN ENJOY A SCENIC TRAIN ROAD OVERLOOKING THE THIRD HIGHEST PEAK IN WEST VIRGINIA.

THE FREE MUSEUM INCLUDES GUIDED TOURS AND DISPLAYS EXPLAINING THE ENGINEERING AND MAINTENANCE OF HISTORIC LOCOMOTIVES.

ONE OF THE LAST MAJOR CIVIL WAR BATTLES TOOK PLACE AT THE NEARBY DROOP MOUNTAIN BATTLEFIELD.

CASS SCENIC RAILROAD STATE PARK ALSO HAS PLACES FOR HIKING, FISHING, BOATING, GOLFING, AND HUNTING.

ADDRESS: 242 MAIN STREET, CASS, WV, UNITED STATES

PASSPORT STAMPS:

NOTES :

Cedar Creek State Park

VISTED DATE :   SPRING ○   SUMMER ○   FALL ○   WINTER ○

WEATHER :   ☀ ○   ⛅ ○   🌧 ○   🌨 ○   ⛈ ○   🌬 ○   🌡 TEMP :

FEE(S) :   RATING : ☆ ☆ ☆ ☆ ☆   WILL I RETURN?   YES / NO

LODGING :   WHO I WENT WITH :

DESCRIPTION / THINGS TO DO :

LOCATED IN CENTRAL WEST VIRGINIA NOT FAR FROM GLENVILLE, CEDAR CREEK STATE PARK OFFERS A PICTURESQUE PLACE TO ENJOY THE GREAT OUTDOORS.

HISTORY BUFFS CAN EXPLORE A FEW GEMS LIKE JOB'S TEMPLE, ONE OF THE STATE'S OLDEST CHURCHES DATING BACK TO 1861.

THE BULLTOWN HISTORIC AREA OFFERS HISTORY REENACTMENTS COMPLETE WITH STAFF DRESSED IN PERIOD CLOTHING.

VISITORS CAN ALSO EXPLORE THE HISTORY CENTER, CIVIL WAR TRENCHES, AND GRAVES.

OUTDOOR ADVENTURES ABOUND AT CEDAR CREEK, AND NATURE LOVERS CAN SPEND THE DAY BOATING HIKING, SWIMMING, AND GOLFING.

THE CAMPGROUND HAS 65 SITES WITH RUNNING WATER AND ELECTRIC HOOKUPS. CAMPERS CAN PURCHASE FIREWOOD AND ICE AT THE SITE CENTER.

ADDRESS: 2947 CEDAR CREEK ROAD, GLENVILLE, WV, UNITED STATES

PASSPORT STAMPS:

NOTES :

Chesapeake and Ohio Canal

VISTED DATE :   SPRING ◯   SUMMER ◯   FALL ◯   WINTER ◯

WEATHER :   ☀ ◯   ⛅ ◯   ☁ ◯   🌨 ◯   ⛈ ◯   🌬 ◯   🌡 TEMP :

FEE(S) :   RATING : ☆ ☆ ☆ ☆ ☆   WILL I RETURN? YES / NO

LODGING :   WHO I WENT WITH :

DESCRIPTION / THINGS TO DO :

THE CHESAPEAKE & OHIO CANAL TAKES GUESTS BACK IN TIME REVEALING THE HISTORY OF THE REGION AND THE COUNTRY'S EARLY METHODS OF TRANSPORTATION.

BUILT IN 1831, THE C&O CANAL, NICKNAMED "THE GRAND OLD DITCH", OPERATED HERE FOR OVER 100 YEARS TRANSPORTING COAL, LUMBER, AND PRODUCE FROM WASHINGTON D.C. TO CUMBERLAND, MARYLAND.

THE CHESAPEAKE & OHIO CANAL HAS BECOME A NATIONAL HISTORICAL PARK. GUESTS CAN COME TO LEARN ABOUT TRANSPORTATION HISTORY AS WELL AS ENJOY THE SURROUNDING NATURAL BEAUTY OF THE REGION.

THE BILLY GOAT TRAIL GIVES IMPRESSIVE VIEWS OF THE POTOMAC RIVER. MEANWHILE, GUESTS CAN ALSO VIEW GREAT FALLS OR ENJOY A BOAT RIDE.

ADDRESS: 205 WEST POTOMAC STREET, WILLIAMSPORT, MD, UNITED STATES

PASSPORT STAMPS:

NOTES :

Chief Logan State Park

VISTED DATE :   SPRING ⚪ SUMMER ⚪ FALL ⚪ WINTER ⚪

WEATHER : ☀️⚪ ⛅⚪ 🌧️⚪ 🌨️⚪ ⛈️⚪ 🌬️⚪   🌡️TEMP :

FEE(S) :   RATING : ☆ ☆ ☆ ☆ ☆   WILL I RETURN? YES / NO

LODGING :   WHO I WENT WITH :

DESCRIPTION / THINGS TO DO :

LOCATED IN LOGAN, WEST VIRGINIA, CHIEF LOGAN STATE PARK SPANS 4,000 ACRES OF THE STATE'S SOUTHERN COALFIELDS.

ALTHOUGH THE PARK HAS PLENTY TO DO OUTDOORS DURING THE WARMER MONTHS, CHIEF LOGAN STATE PARK HAS 600 MILES OF PROPERTY ALLOWING ATV-RIDERS TO TAKE THE QUADS OUT FOR A DAY OF EXPLORING.

DURING HUNTING SEASON, SPORTSMEN CAN COME TO HUNT FOR DEER, GROUSE, TURKEYS, AND WATERFOWL.

THE CAMPGROUND ACCOMMODATES 40 UNITS IN TOTAL, BUT ONLY 26 HAVE FULL WATER, ELECTRIC, AND SEWAGE HOOKUPS.

ADDRESS: 376 LITTLE BUFFALO CREEK ROAD, LOGAN, WV, UNITED STATES

PASSPORT STAMPS:

NOTES :

Harpers Ferry

WEATHER : ☀ ○ ⛅ ○ 🌧 ○ 🌨 ○ ⛈ ○ 🌬 ○   🌡 TEMP :

FEE(S) :   RATING : ☆ ☆ ☆ ☆ ☆   WILL I RETURN? YES / NO

LODGING :   WHO I WENT WITH :

DESCRIPTION / THINGS TO DO :

SITUATED AT THE INTERSECTION OF THE POTOMAC AND SHENANDOAH RIVERS, HARPERS FERRY OFFERS A MIXTURE OF HISTORY AND NATURE IN A QUAINT MOUNTAIN VILLAGE.

THIS CHARMING, SMALL TOWN IN THE LOWER SHENANDOAH VALLEY TAKES ITS NAME FROM THE ROBERT HARPER, A MAN WHO USED TO RUN A FERRY THERE IN THE 18TH CENTURY.

DURING THE CIVIL WAR, IT BECAME THE NORTHERNMOST POST CONTROLLED BY THE CONFEDERATE ARMY.

THE LOWER PORTION OF HARPERS FERRY FORMS PART OF THE HARPERS FERRY NATIONAL HISTORICAL PARK.

VISITORS CAN COME TO ENJOY HIKING AND BIKING TRAILS.

THE HISTORICAL HARPERS FERRY CONTAINS MUSEUMS, SHOPS, AND EATERIES BESIDE THE BEAUTIFUL BLUE RIDGE MOUNTAINS.

ADDRESS: 171 SHORELINE DRIVE, HARPERS FERRY, WV, UNITED STATES

PASSPORT STAMPS:

NOTES :

Gauley River

VISTED DATE :   SPRING ◯ SUMMER ◯ FALL ◯ WINTER ◯

WEATHER : ☀◯ ⛅◯ 🌧◯ 🌨◯ ⛈◯ 🌬◯   🌡 TEMP :

FEE(S) :   RATING : ☆ ☆ ☆ ☆ ☆   WILL I RETURN? YES / NO

LODGING :   WHO I WENT WITH :

DESCRIPTION / THINGS TO DO :

THRILL-SEEKERS CAN'T PASS UP A VISIT TO GAULEY RIVER, ONE OF THE STATE'S BEST LOCATIONS FOR WHITE WATER RAFTING.

GAULEY RIVER RUNS 25 MILES IN ADDITION TO THE 6-MILE LONG MEADOW RIVER.

A BOAT TRIP PROVIDES BREATHTAKING VIEWS OF THE TERRAIN WITH PICTURESQUE GORGES AND VALLEYS.

ALONG THE WAY, VISITORS CAN SPOT LOCAL WILDLIFE LIKE WHITE-TAILED DEER, VIEW RARE PLANT SPECIES, AND ADMIRE THE WOODLANDS OF OAK, BEECH, HEMLOCK, AND DOGWOOD.

VIGOROUS CLASS V+ RAPIDS MAKE THIS AN EXCELLENT CHOICE FOR THE ADVENTUROUS.

CONFEDERATE AND UNION FORCES CLASHED AT THE NEARBY CARNIFEX FERRY BATTLEFIELD STATE PARK IN 1861.

ADDRESS: GAULEY RIVER NATIONAL RECREATION AREA, GLEN JEAN, WV, UNITED STATES

PASSPORT STAMPS:

NOTES :

Made in the USA
Middletown, DE
11 December 2022

18032885R00060